KENNETH C. DAVIS
ILLUSTRATED BY ROB SHEPPERSON

DON'T
KNOW
MUCH
ABOUT

George
Washington

HarperCollins*Publishers*

Photo and Map Credits:

Page 65, All rights reserved, The Metropolitan Museum of Art, gift of John Stewart Kennedy, 1897 (97.34). All other photographs courtesy of the Library of Congress.

Maps on pages 11 and 57 by Patricia Tobin.

This is a Don't Know Much About® book.
Don't Know Much About® is the trademark of Kenneth C. Davis.

Don't Know Much About® George Washington

Copyright © 2003 by Kenneth C. Davis

www.harperchildrens.com

Library of Congress Cataloging-in-Publication Data
Davis, Kenneth C.
    Don't know much about George Washington / Kenneth C. Davis ;
illustrated by Rob Shepperson.
        p.   cm. — (Don't know much about)
    Summary: Examines the childhood and youth, education, early surveying career, life in the military, and presidency of George Washington.
    ISBN 0-06-442124-4 (pbk.) — ISBN 0-06-028817-5 (lib. bdg.)
    1. Washington, George, 1732–1799—Miscellanea—Juvenile literature. 2. Presidents—United States—Miscellanea—Juvenile literature.   [1. Washington, George, 1732–1799. 2. Presidents.   3. Questions and answers.]   I. Shepperson, Rob, ill.   II. Title.
E312.66 .D39   2003   973.4'1'092—dc21   [B]   2002068729

Design by Charles Yuen
1 2 3 4 5 6 7 8 9 10
❖
First Edition

ACKNOWLEDGMENTS

An author's name goes on the cover of a book. But behind that book are a great many people who make it all happen. I would like to thank all of the wonderful people at HarperCollins who helped make this book a reality, including Susan Katz, Kate Morgan Jackson, Barbara Lalicki, Harriett Barton, Rosemary Brosnan, Meredith Charpentier, Amy Burton, Dana Hayward, Maggie Herold, Jeanne Hogle, Fumi Kosaka, Rachel Orr, Donna Lifshotz, and Robina Khalid. I would also like to thank David Black, Joy Tutela, and Alix Reid for their friendship, assistance, and great ideas. My wife, Joann, and my children, Jenny and Colin, are always a source of inspiration, joy, and support, and without them my work would not be possible.

I especially thank Kevin P. Kelly, historian at Colonial Williamsburg Foundation, for reviewing the manuscript and providing helpful insights; Rob Shepperson for his clever illustrations; and Barry Varela for his hard work and unique contribution.

CONTENTS

George
Washington,
painted by
Gilbert Stuart
in 1796

*H*e is probably in your pocket right now. Go ahead and check. If you have a dollar bill or a quarter, then George Washington is in your pocket.

It is very hard to go anywhere in America and not be reminded of George Washington. Our nation's capital is named after him, and one of its most familiar landmarks was built in his honor. He is the only president with a whole state named after him. And all across America, there are thousands of towns, streets, squares, and schools named for George Washington. In many classrooms, there is a picture of Washington hanging on the wall, perhaps alongside that of Abraham Lincoln, another great American president. It is Washington and Lincoln, whose birthdays are in February, whom we celebrate every year on Presidents' Day.

So George Washington—the leader of the army that won America's independence from Great Britain and America's first elected president—is certainly one of the most famous Americans. But who was he? What was he like? How did he grow up? Perhaps more than any other American, George Washington has inspired stories, legends, and myths. He was a good little boy who never told a lie, even when he cut down his father's cherry tree. He was so strong he could toss a coin across a wide river. He didn't smile in his portrait because he had wooden teeth.

There are elements of truth behind these stories, some of which were made up long after Washington died. Washington was very honest, by most accounts, and he did wear false teeth. But those stories are not who George Washington really was. And you know what? The real person and the things he did are much more interesting than those made-up stories.

This book tells the remarkable true story of the extraordinary life and times of the man who was once called the "indispensable American." That means, without George Washington, there would have been no America. And it tells that story by asking questions about a real person who wasn't perfect.

The Don't Know Much About® series is about questions. And it is about real people. Asking real questions about real people is one way to get the true story of George Washington, the real man who was "first in the hearts of his countrymen."

CHAPTER 1

The Wild, Wild East

Was the "Father of the Country" born in America?

Yes and no. When George Washington was born on February 22, 1732, the United States of America did not exist. Like most babies of that day, George was born at home, in a brick farmhouse on Bridges Creek near the Potomac River in Virginia.

At that time Virginia was still a colony of Great Britain. A powerful empire, Great Britain was made up of England, Scotland, Wales, and Ireland, along with colonies in America, India, and other parts of the world. All of this was ruled by England's king, who controlled the empire along with the British Parliament, the group of men in London, England, who passed laws, much the way America's Congress does today.

Like many people in Virginia and the other colonies in America, the Washingtons considered themselves Englishmen loyal to the English throne. George's great-grandfather John Washington had left England for America in 1657 and married the daughter of a tobacco planter. Almost since the time the first Englishmen came to America, growing tobacco had been the fastest way to make a fortune in Virginia.

George's grandfather Lawrence also grew tobacco and married a woman with more tobacco land.

WHAT DOES IT MEAN?

A **colony** is a group of people who have moved to a far-off territory but who still retain ties with the parent country; also, colony can mean the territory itself.

Was George Washington an only child?

George Washington's father, Augustine, or Gus, was also a tobacco farmer. Like many Virginians, Gus worked hard and prospered. Before George was born, Gus added to his family's holdings by building a small ironworks. Gus married Jane Butler, and they had two sons, Lawrence and Augustine Jr. But in 1730 Jane died of a fever. About a year later Gus married Mary Ball, the twenty-three-year-old daughter of another tobacco planter. Eleven months after the wedding, George Washington was born.

When George was three, his father moved the family to a new home, Little Hunting Creek Plantation. A few years later they moved again to Ferry Farm on the Rappahannock River opposite the village of Fredericksburg. By that time George and his two older half brothers had been joined by four other children: Elizabeth, Samuel, John Augustine, or Jack, and Charles. Another sister, Mildred, was born in 1739 but died the following year. Large families and death in infancy were not unusual in colonial times. And many women, as many as one in eight, died while giving birth. Curiously little

WHAT DOES IT MEAN?

A **plantation** is a large farm on which crops such as tobacco, sugar, or cotton are grown; in colonial America, most plantations were worked by slaves.

is known of Washington's siblings, except for Lawrence, and they played almost no role in their brother's career. George also never had much to say or write about his father, who was often away from the family on business.

About his mother George Washington had mixed feelings. While Washington always showed her respect, Mary Ball Washington was known as a tough, bossy woman who smoked a corncob pipe and seemed to inspire fear among Washington's friends. As an adult Washington didn't visit her very often, never invited her to his home, and never introduced her to his wife.

THE THIRTEEN ORIGINAL COLONIES		
New Hampshire	New Jersey	North Carolina
Massachusetts	Pennsylvania	South Carolina
Rhode Island	Delaware	Georgia
Connecticut	Maryland	
New York	Virginia	

Was George Washington's family rich?

The Washingtons were well-off, but they were not very rich or powerful. George's father, Augustine, owned several plantations totaling around ten thousand acres. About fifty slaves worked in the fields and farm buildings, raising tobacco and other crops. Tobacco was the main source of income—the Washingtons sold it to merchants who shipped it to Great Britain. With the money earned from tobacco, the Washingtons bought things—such as sugar, tea, and spices—that couldn't be grown in Virginia.

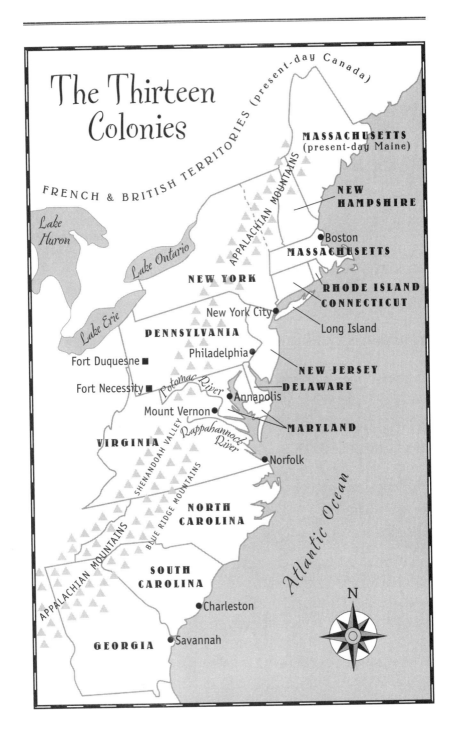

Ten thousand acres may sound like a lot of land, but in Virginia back then the truly wealthy owned hundreds of thousands of acres. Many of the richest Virginians were descended from aristocrats who had owned vast properties back in England. These aristocratic, wealthy families were known as the "First Families" of Virginia. Washington's ancestors had not been wealthy, and during George's childhood the Washingtons were not considered one of these First Families.

Was America big and powerful when George Washington was born?

Not at all. The British colonies in North America were strung out in a narrow strip along the Atlantic coast. A couple of hundred miles inland, the deep forests were still being explored by Europeans. The only people who lived there were Indians.

In the 1730s the total population of colonial America was about 650,000; almost 100,000 of those people were African-American slaves. Great Britain's population, by contrast, was more than six million.

What's so good about owning a colony anyway?

Having control of a whole continent, especially a big one like North America, when you live on a small island like the English did, is a very profitable venture. First, there are all those valuable natural resources like wood from America's forests. Then there are those wonderful things that Americans grew so well like tobacco, sugar, and other goodies the English enjoyed.

But even more important was the fact that the colonists in America liked to buy things from "back home" in England. The colonial Americans, mostly English people by birth or family connections, wanted to live like Englishmen rather than Indians. While the Indians had lived well and happily in America for thousands of years without fine clothes, expensive furniture, sherry, and tea, many Americans preferred to live in the British style. As cities grew and Americans began to prosper, British merchants knew there was plenty of money to be made selling their goods in America.

But just selling things to Americans wasn't enough for the British government. So the English Parliament started to pass laws that placed limits on what Americans could buy and sell. For instance, they said that Americans could only sell their products like tobacco and wool to the British. That meant the Americans could not get a higher price from someone else like France or Spain. Then Parliament decided that anything the colonies wanted to buy had to be transported aboard British ships, which meant that Americans were forced to pay what British shippers demanded. Parliament also started to pass a set of taxes called tariffs on anything that Americans wanted to buy from another country like Spain or the Netherlands. These laws hurt Americans because they made everything more expensive and limited the amount that American merchants could earn from selling their products. To make matters worse, Americans had very little say in making these laws, which were passed by men across an ocean, thousands of miles away back in London, who didn't really care what Americans thought.

Would George's father and mother have liked these restrictions on trade?

We can't say for sure how Augustine and Mary Washington felt about anything. They weren't famous, and no one wrote down what they said. We can guess, however, that they felt much as their neighbors did—that Parliament's laws were unfair. In fact, the Washingtons probably defied the laws, quietly, when they could. It was all well and good for Parliament to *tell* colonists they couldn't sell their tobacco to Dutch traders; but Britain was an ocean away, and enforcing the law was difficult.

Today, does anybody believe the old tale about young George and the cherry tree?

Shortly after Washington died, a man named Mason Locke Weems wrote a book called *A History of the Life and Death, Virtues and Exploits, of General George Washington*. Parson Weems (*parson* is an old-fashioned word for clergyman, minister, or pastor) wanted to show that a great man like Washington had had no faults, even as a child.

One of the stories Parson Weems told was that young George chopped down his father's cherry tree. When his father asked who had done it, George said, "I can't tell a lie. I did cut it with my hatchet."

The problem is that there's no evidence that anything like that ever happened. It's made up, just like the story about Washington throwing a coin across the Rappahannock River.

What did George and his friends wear? There was no Gap or Old Navy in George's day.

As infants and toddlers, children wore:

- clout — a diaper made of linen and either tied or pinned (carefully!) with straight pins.

- bed gown — a long, shapeless gown, open down the front, worn by babies.

- pudding cap — a padded cap for the head of a child learning to walk. Basically, a crash helmet for toddlers. Colonials believed that repeated blows to the head would cause the brain to go soft like pudding. A common pet name for toddlers was "puddinghead."

- leading-string bands — like the leashes you sometimes see on today's toddlers, leading-string bands were sewn to the shoulders of children's gowns so their parents could keep tabs on them. Older girls sometimes wore leading-string bands as a symbol of their need for guidance.

- stays — strips of bone, reed, or other rigid material used to stiffen a corset, which was a kind of tight-fitting undershirt. Stays were supposed to support the rib cage and improve posture. Boys wore them from toddlerhood to about age seven. Girls wore them all their lives.

Older children wore:

- child's gown — a back-fastening gown worn by girls until about age twelve or fourteen, and by boys until they were breeched (see next item). Boys' gowns sometimes buttoned up the front to resemble a man's long coat.

- breeches — grown-up pants. At about seven years old, boys would have their breeching—they would be given their adult clothes. Childhood was over when a boy was breeched.

Did getting breeches mean you had to go to work?

Going from gown to breeches was a big day for a colonial boy. But it didn't mean he was now an adult. For George it would mean taking on more chores around the plantations Little Hunting Creek and Ferry Farm, where he grew up. He would no longer be the one taken care of—it was time for him to start pulling his own weight at home.

What did colonial kids do for fun?

There were no televisions. No computers. No videos or video games. No electronic gadgets of any kind. There were no fancy dolls or action figures or sports equipment.

Children played with simple, handmade toys. Dolls might be fashioned out of wood or dried corn husks. A drum, a kite, or a spyglass (that is, a small telescope) might be a child's most treasured possession. A jackknife was a boy's best friend, for with a knife a child could carve other toys out of wood.

And, of course, there were no soccer teams or Little Leagues. Kids had to make their own fun. Boys went fishing and hunting. Girls did needlepoint and quilted. Kids swam in rivers and ponds. They rode horses. They read the Bible, especially the exciting parts, like Daniel in the lion's den.

Were there other games that kids today might play?

Sure there were. Some other games eighteenth-century boys and girls played were:

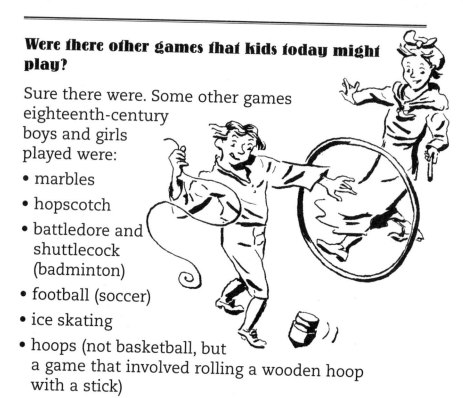

- marbles
- hopscotch
- battledore and shuttlecock (badminton)
- football (soccer)
- ice skating
- hoops (not basketball, but a game that involved rolling a wooden hoop with a stick)
- ninepins (a form of bowling)
- pegtop (played with a top spun by a string)
- fives (a game like handball)

How did George first acquire land of his own?

When George was eleven, in 1743, his father died of a fever, leaving him Ferry Farm and some other land, as well as ten slaves. It might seem strange that an eleven-year-old could become owner of his own plantation, but much was expected of children in those days. George would have worked alongside his father for a number of years, learning how to run the plantation. He also would have had several years of formal education, learning the "three R's"— reading, 'riting, and 'rithmetic. Whether he attended a schoolhouse or, more likely, received tutoring at home, isn't known.

At the time of Augustine Washington's death, George's older half brother Lawrence inherited the larger plantation at Little Hunting Creek on the Potomac. Lawrence later renamed the plantation Mount Vernon, in honor of Admiral Edward Vernon, under whom he had served in the British navy.

How is a skunk like a squash?

Both *skunk* and *squash* come from Indian words. When Europeans first came to the Americas, they found many plants and animals they had never before seen. Hard to believe, but Europeans didn't know about corn, potatoes, tomatoes, and chocolate. In fact, the words *maize* (another word for corn), *potato*, *tomato*, and *chocolate* all come from Indian languages.

Other words in English that come from Indian languages include:

succotash	woodchuck	hammock
barbecue	moose	hurricane
hickory	caribou	toboggan
pecan	terrapin	canoe
cashew	possum	
tobacco	coyote	
chipmunk		
raccoon		

All of these things were new to Europeans.

Where did George Washington go to college?

Nowhere. George Washington never went to college. Few people went to college in America back then. There were only a handful of universities in America and only one in Virginia—the College of William and Mary in Williamsburg, Virginia's colonial capital. Unlike his older half brothers, who had been sent to England for school, George had little formal education. One story has it that his father hired a one-eyed convict to teach him his letters. Another story said he went to a school run by a local minister.

George had only a few years of real school, getting some of the Latin and Greek grammar that "grammar school" drilled into boys back then. Of course, most girls were not sent to school but were taught to read at home, if at all, where they were also learning how to cook, sew, and manage a house. George did study science, geography, history, and math—at which he was a bit of a whiz. He supposedly loved to count stairs and windowpanes in houses. Once he calculated that there were 71,000 seeds in a pound of red clover.

What was George like as a young man?

Three years after his father died, fourteen-year-old George went to live with his older half brother Lawrence at Mount Vernon. Lawrence had married Anne Fairfax, the daughter of one of Virginia's wealthiest men, and George was introduced to the world of Virginia's true upper-class society. Like most young men, George liked to dance and sing, to

"LET NOT YOUR MORSELS BE TOO BIG FOR THE JOWLS"

One thing he did learn was manners. As part of his studies, the sixteen-year-old George copied down 110 lessons from a book called *Rules of Civility & Decent Behaviour in Company and Conversation*. Here are some of them:

1. Every action done in company ought to be done with some sign of respect to those that are present.

5. If you cough, sneeze, sigh, or yawn, do it not loud but privately.

15. Keep your nails clean and short, also your hands and teeth clean yet without showing any great concern for them.

22. Show not yourself glad at the misfortune of another, though he were your enemy.

97. Put not another bite into your mouth till the former be swallowed; let not your morsels be too big for the jowls.

110. Labour to keep alive in your breast that little spark of celestial fire called Conscience.

laugh and joke. He had crushes on a few local girls but no real girlfriend, which is a little curious. He was pretty wealthy, smart, tall, and physically impressive. Some people thought he was too serious; he was not exactly lighthearted. And from the earliest age, he seemed to have a strong sense of duty and honor, which were important ideas in the eighteenth century. Duty called him to serve—his family, friends, and country, which still meant England. Honor demanded that people think well of him, so he set extremely high standards for himself.

It probably wasn't easy to be George Washington as a teenager. But his devotion to duty and honor would serve him well in later life.

CHAPTER 2

Action on the Western Front

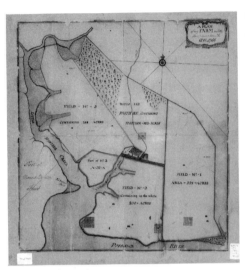

Washington's survey of his farm on Little Hunting Creek

What was George Washington's first job?

Living with Lawrence was perfect for the teenage Washington. He could ride, hunt, and fish to his heart's delight. But in colonial times, teenagers were practically adults and had to think about the rest of their lives. For young George Washington, there were few options, and it was clear that more school was not his first choice. Running the small property he had inherited at Ferry Farm didn't hold much interest for George either, especially since that was where his mother ruled. One of the only other options for young men at the time was a military career.

Lawrence thought George should join the British navy. But Mary Washington still had say over her son's future, and Washington's mother put her foot down. She realized that, as a young colonial, George would probably not get very far in the Royal Navy. His British superiors would most likely look down at young Americans, who were viewed back in England as "country cousins." She may not have been the most loving mother, but in this case she was smart enough to steer George in the right direction.

With his passion for math and the Virginia woods, George began to learn the basics of surveying, an important job in a big country with few cities, roads, or street signs, and very few reliable maps. A surveyor traveled the countryside, using a chain measure made up of one hundred flexible links, a compass, and other tools to measure plots of land, mark boundaries of property, and draw useful maps. Surveying was the perfect job for a young man with a mind for numbers and a love for horses and the outdoors. By surveying his property and that of his neighbors, George Washington was earning 125 British pounds a year by the time he was eighteen— that was more than most farmers made in that time.

Did George Washington want to grow up to be a soldier?

Not at all. He was far happier as a surveyor. But George Washington was still ambitious, and surveying other people's land was only part of the answer. Ferry Farm, which he inherited from his father, was too small to make him rich. Through his half brother Lawrence, George had also been introduced to the world of the upper class of Virginia society and wanted to be part of it. When Lawrence married Anne Fairfax, he had joined one of the most powerful families in Virginia. The Fairfaxes claimed more than five million acres of Virginia farmland. With their great wealth, the Fairfaxes were one of the most important families in America, members (as was Lawrence) of Virginia's *House of Burgesses*. George knew them all and was eventually introduced to the head of the family from England, Thomas, Lord Fairfax.

> **WHAT DOES IT MEAN?**
>
> Burgesses were elected officials whose function was similar to that of our state representatives. Created in 1619, the Virginia **House of Burgesses** was the first legislature, or body of elected representatives who meet to write laws, in the colonies.

What kind of West was this?

In those days colonial settlements ended at the Blue Ridge Mountains in the western part of what is now Virginia. Beyond the mountains was thickly forested, mostly unmapped wilderness—wilderness that, in theory at least, the Fairfax family owned. The problem for Lord Fairfax was that anyone who wanted to could move onto the Fairfaxes' western lands and squat there. (To "squat" means to live in a place that doesn't belong to you.) It was impossible to keep settlers off the land, and if the land wasn't even mapped, who was to say who owned it? And of course the Fairfaxes didn't receive any rent from squatters. They needed a surveyor to map out the land into official plots that could then be rented out or sold. Squatters would become renters or purchasers, and the Fairfaxes would make money from the land.

Did he see sagebrush and cactuses?

When he was sixteen, George crossed the Blue Ridge Mountains with George William Fairfax and a team of surveyors. They roamed up and down the Shenandoah Valley, taking measurements and marking plots of land. They saw no sagebrush or cactuses, but they did meet a war party of Indians ("with only one scalp," as Washington put it in his diary). Luckily for the two Georges, this group of Indians was on friendly terms with the English.

The next year, at only seventeen years of age, George was appointed head surveyor of Culpeper County in northern Virginia. He spent about three years, on and off, surveying the western frontier. It was a hard life—all day walking or riding on horseback in the hot sun, the rain, the snow.

Did George's hard work pay off?

Yes. With the money he earned as a surveyor, George bought up hundreds of acres of prime western land. The land might not produce income right away, but over time it would only become more valuable. Washington knew that settlement of the West was inevitable. The wilderness that he bought cheap would command a high price someday as farmland. He was right about that.

Washington had shown Lord Fairfax that he was trustworthy, intelligent, and strong. And so, perhaps most important, he had in Lord Fairfax earned a powerful *patron*—that is, a friend and supporter—who could assist him in his budding career.

❝ We got our Supper and was lighted into a Room and not being so good a Woodsman as ye rest of my Company stripped myself very orderly and went into ye Bed as they called it to my Surprize I found it to be nothing but a Little Straw-Matted together without sheets or anything else but only one thread Bear blanket with double its weight of Vermin such as Lice, Fleas &c. I was glad to get up. . . . I put on my Cloths and lay as my Companions. Had we not been very tired I am sure we should not have slep'd much that night I made a Promise not to Sleep so from that time forward, chusing rather to sleep in ye open Air before a fire. **❞**

—**George Washington**, in a diary entry written during his first trip into the wilderness

Why did George take a Caribbean vacation?

In 1751 George took a break from surveying to sail to the island of Barbados with his half brother Lawrence. But it wasn't for the sand and surf. Lawrence was sick with consumption—what is now called tuberculosis—and he believed the warm Caribbean climate would do his lungs good.

Unfortunately, Lawrence did not get better and, to make matters worse, George caught smallpox, an often deadly disease. George survived and sailed back to Virginia. The next year Lawrence, too, returned to Mount Vernon, but died soon after. His widow, Anne Fairfax Washington, inherited the plantation. When she died in 1761, Mount Vernon went to George. For the rest of his life he would think of it as his true home.

> ### A Pox Upon You!
>
> Many diseases that are virtually unknown in the United States today, such as malaria, yellow fever, scarlet fever, typhus, and smallpox, were common in colonial America. Infectious diseases such as chicken pox, measles, and mumps were especially dangerous, killing young and old alike.
>
> In contrast, diseases of old age were relatively rare—few individuals lived long enough to come down with them!

When did George Washington enlist in the army?

Shortly after Lawrence died, George was appointed to the rank of major in the Virginia militia. At only twenty years of age, Washington was put in charge of one of four Virginia military districts. His job was to train the officers who would then train the soldiers.

But Washington himself had never been trained as an officer. In fact, he had no military background at all. How had he won this position, which came, by the way, with a generous salary?

Although Washington wasn't yet a military man, he was an expert hunter and horseman. He was a physically impressive man, large and strong, and his time on the frontier had toughened both his body and his mind. Washington was a natural commander: When he talked, people listened. And most important of all, Washington was friends with Colonel Fairfax, who was an advisor to Governor Dinwiddie of Virginia. Fairfax pulled strings, and Washington got the job he wanted.

Now, the job he wanted—training officers—was one he didn't know how to do. He solved that problem by hiring someone else to do the job for him—at half the pay he was receiving.

COLONIALS AND REDCOATS

There were two kinds of armies in colonial America. The first kind was made up of colonials. Each of the thirteen colonies trained, supplied, and manned an army for its own defense in times of crisis. It was over colonial forces—a Virginia regiment—that Washington was given command in 1754.

The second kind of military force was the royal army, manned by officers from Britain—called Redcoats, for the color of their uniforms. When a colonial army worked together with a royal army, the colonial officers always took orders from their Redcoat counterparts, regardless of their relative ranks. In other words, a lowly Redcoat captain could command a colonial general!

Who were the colonials preparing to fight?

The French and their Indian allies.

Both Britain and France held possessions in North America. Britain had its colonies on the Eastern seaboard. France had settlements in what is now

Canada, as well as at New Orleans. There were also some French forts in the Great Lakes region of what is now the United States.

The French were mainly trappers, traders, and soldiers. Most were not in America with their families to settle down.

Indians viewed the British as the gravest threat to their way of life. The British outnumbered the French twenty to one and cleared land rather than merely trapping on it. Therefore, most Indians sided with the French in their conflict with the British.

Why did Washington pay a visit to a French fort?

In 1753 the French built a small fort on the south side of Lake Erie, in what is now Pennsylvania. Governor Dinwiddie of Virginia viewed the French fort as the first step toward an attempt by the French to take over all lands west of the Appalachian Mountains.

Dinwiddie ordered twenty-one-year-old Washington to tell the French commander that the fort was on Virginia property and that the French must leave. After many adventures—he rode through hostile territory in terrible weather—Washington delivered the message. The French commander promptly ignored it, of course. The French would not be kicked out of the area without a fight.

Washington returned to Virginia and published an account of his travels. The book proved popular in both England and the colonies and helped spread the fame of the young soldier.

❝ Before we were halfway over, we were jammed in the ice in such a manner that we expected every moment our raft 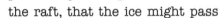 to sink, and ourselves to perish. I put out my setting pole to try to stop the raft, that the ice might pass by, when the rapidity of the stream threw it with so much violence against the pole, that it jerked me out into ten feet of water, but I fortunately saved myself by catching hold of one of the raft logs. Notwithstanding all our efforts we could not get the raft to either shore, but were obliged, as we were near an island, to quit our raft and make to it.

"The cold was so extremely severe, that [my companion] had all his fingers, and some of his toes frozen, and the water was shut up so hard, that we found no difficulty in getting off the island on the ice in the morning. ❞

—From *The Journal of Major George Washington, Sent by the Hon. Robert Dinwiddie to the Commandant of the French Forces in Ohio*

How did George Washington start a war?

Washington's tale of his first adventure made him a minor celebrity in Virginia and London. But his reports of his experience with the French also convinced the governor of Virginia that the French were going to continue to be a problem for the

British. Even though the two countries were at peace, there was much talk of a war to come between these European superpowers.

In the spring of 1754, Governor Dinwiddie sent Washington back into the wilderness to help complete a new fort and defend it from French attack. Before Washington arrived, he learned he was too late. The French had already attacked the unfinished fort, captured the men building it, and begun a fort of their own called Fort Duquesne. Then the French sent a small group of soldiers to attack Washington. Warned about this French raiding party by an Indian named Chief Half-King, Washington readied his men, and on the morning of May 28, 1754, he attacked the French soldiers. With the help of Half-King's warriors, Washington's men killed ten French soldiers and captured another twenty-two.

Without knowing it, George Washington had ordered the first shots in a war that would spread from the backwoods of America to all of Europe.

AMERICAN VOICES

"I can assure you. I heard Bullets whistle and believe me there was something charming in the sound. **"**
—**George Washington,** describing his first battle in a letter to his brother Jack

What was the Seven Years' War?

Europe was very different hundreds of years ago. For many years France and Austria had battled for control of central Europe. France also had a powerful navy and challenged Britain for control of the seas.

For this reason Britain traditionally had sided with Austria against France.

Britain and Prussia, a powerful Germanic state, agreed to protect a small country called Hanover from invaders. Although they were traditional enemies, Austria and France feared the British-Prussian alliance and decided to team up.

In 1756 war broke out all over Europe. There was no Germany then, so basically, it was France, Russia, Sweden, Saxony, and Austria against Britain, Prussia, and Hanover. The conflict came to be known as the Seven Years' War.

Why did Washington resign his command?

After the skirmish near Fort Duquesne, Washington was hailed as a hero. Governor Dinwiddie promoted him to full colonel and named him commander of the Virginia regiment.

Washington's run of good fortune soon ended. Fort Duquesne was still held by the French. Washington quickly built a new outpost, Fort Necessity, in southwestern Pennsylvania. Several weeks later, on the morning of July 3, four hundred French soldiers attacked the three hundred soldiers stationed at

Fort Necessity. By late afternoon, with a third of his soldiers dead or wounded, Washington was forced to surrender. The French allowed him and his men to retreat to Virginia.

It was a humiliating defeat for the British. Governor Dinwiddie threatened to demote Washington to captain. Rather than accept the demotion, Washington resigned his command.

How did Washington regain his command?

Despite having resigned from the Virginia regiment, Washington was not yet ready to retire from the military. Instead he applied to be an aide to General Edward Braddock, commander of the royal forces.

Although Washington held no official position, General Braddock trusted him and listened to his advice. In the summer of 1755, the royal army's mission was to take Fort Duquesne and chase the French out of British territory.

Braddock's campaign was a complete disaster. In a battle outside Fort Duquesne, nearly four hundred British soldiers, including Braddock himself, lost their lives, and another five hundred were wounded. The Redcoats were forced to retreat in utter defeat.

Washington, however, came out of the battle covered in glory. While other men fled, he rode up

How to Build a Colonial Fort

1. Choose a hilltop or other easily defensible area.

2. Clear it of brush and trees.

3. Decide how big and in what shape you want your fort to be. Fort Necessity was roughly circular and was about fifty-three feet across.

4. Dig a trench about two feet deep all the way around in the shape of your fort.

5. Cut down a bunch of logs. Split them in half and then cut them into nine-foot lengths, with a point on one end.

6. Stick the logs pointy-end up in the trench. Your stockade fence will be about seven feet high. Pack the logs into the ground securely. Fill in any gaps between the logs with smaller, flat-tipped logs about four feet high. These can be used as gun rests.

7. Go back and cut some more logs. You don't have nearly enough to make it all the way around.

8. Remember to include at least one door.

9. Congratulations. You have just built a simple stockade fort. You can add a small storage shed inside. And it's probably a good idea to dig some trenches around the stockade, for extra protection. Hurry up—your scouts say the enemy is only a day's march away!

and down the battle line, urging his comrades on. Four bullets pierced his coat, but amazingly none wounded him. Two horses were shot from beneath him. He had proven himself to be extraordinarily brave (and lucky!).

Back in Virginia, the news of Washington's bravery made him a hero once again. Governor Dinwiddie, under pressure from the House of Burgesses, offered Washington his old command, which he accepted.

Did Washington ever take Fort Duquesne?

For the next three years, Washington patrolled the Virginia frontier, protecting colonials from French and Native American attack. He scored no great triumphs but suffered no great defeats either. Finally, in the fall of 1758, Washington, along with five thousand troops under the command of a British general named Forbes, captured Fort Duquesne without a fight.

Although Virginia was now safe from invasion by the French, the capture of Fort Duquesne (renamed Fort Pitt, later Pittsburgh) was something of a hollow victory. Washington had borne hardship and illness. He was worn out. His home, Mount Vernon, was falling into neglect. He had had enough of the soldier's life. Once again he resigned from the army.

The French and Indian War would drag on for another four years, though Virginia wouldn't be threatened again. The war would end with the British conquest of Canada. But Washington would see no more action in it. He would return to Mount Vernon, to live the peaceful life of a planter.

CHAPTER 3

Citizen Washington

The marriage of George Washington and Martha Custis

Who was Sally Fairfax?

Sally Fairfax was the wife of Washington's old friend George William Fairfax. Over the years Washington had spent countless evenings with the Fairfaxes at their huge estate, Belvoir. Similarly they had visited him at Mount Vernon time and again. Slowly Washington had fallen in love with his friend's wife, as he confessed, in a roundabout way, in this letter to her from 1758:

> 'Tis true I profess myself a votary to Love. I acknowledge that a Lady is in the case; and, further, I confess that this lady is known to you. . . .

Misconstrue not my meaning, 'tis obvious;
doubt it not or expose it. The world has no
business to know the object of my love,
declared in this manner to—you, when I want
to conceal it.

Washington knew the romance was hopeless,
however, and concluded the letter with a resigned
tone: "But adieu to this till happier times, if ever I
shall see them." Sally Fairfax appears never to have
returned his feelings, or even to have acknowledged
that they existed.

Who was Mrs. Daniel Parke Custis?

At home in Mount Vernon

Martha Dandridge was born in 1731 to a comfortable
but not very rich Virginia family. Like most girls of
the day, she did not receive much formal
schooling—she could barely read. Short and plump,
she was not a great beauty.

But Martha grew up to be intelligent, gracious, and
good-natured. She married Daniel Parke Custis, a
very wealthy Virginia planter. Martha and Daniel
had two surviving children, Jack and Patsy.

Washington met Martha Custis not long after her husband died. Her virtues—kindheartedness, respectability, modesty—appealed to him, and he began courting her.

The courtship was brief—they met only a few times, in the fall of 1758, before marrying. In those days, especially among the upper crust, marriage was often seen as something of a business arrangement. For Washington, Martha's considerable fortune made her a good match. In the young colonel, Martha Custis saw a reputable and reliable stepfather for her two children.

Washington and Martha Custis married on January 6, 1759. Jack and Patsy became Washington's stepchildren. With Martha's property added to his own, Washington was now one of the wealthiest men in Virginia.

Did the new husband practice the new husbandry?

Yes, but not at first. *Husbandry* simply means farming or agriculture. For many years Washington lived as a typical Virginia planter, but he became intrigued by the "new husbandry," which referred to a set of methods designed to increase crop yields and preserve the land. These innovations included crop rotation (planting first one crop, then the next year another in a single field), fertilization, deeper plowing, and planting in rows instead of scattering seed willy-nilly.

Washington was a firm believer in the new husbandry. He had seen the way tobacco, in particular, quickly wore out fields, leaving them useless. During the 1760s, Washington stopped growing tobacco, which for generations had been a major source of wealth in Virginia. Instead he started planting wheat, which he rotated with buckwheat, grass, and clover. These alternate crops were plowed back into the land to renew it.

Mount Vernon never brought in much profit—the soil wasn't as fertile as that of Washington's properties farther south and west. But unlike many of his neighbors on the Potomac, Washington didn't ruin his land.

Who worked the fields of Mount Vernon?

African-American slaves. Washington had inherited slaves from his father, and Martha, too, had owned slaves. These slaves planted, maintained, and harvested the crops. They also worked as house servants, cooks, carpenters, cobblers, barrelmakers, blacksmiths, and coachmen. They worked six days a week, from sunup to sundown.

How did Washington, champion of liberty, feel about slavery?

As a young man, Washington seems not to have been too troubled by slavery. He had been born into a slaveholding family. His friends and neighbors owned slaves. Slavery was part of the world as he found it.

As he aged and became more devoted to the cause of freedom, Washington did begin to recognize the inconsistency of his position. How could he and other slaveholding Patriots insist that "all men are created equal" and yet hold other men in bondage?

We must ask the question, too. Were the Founding Fathers just hypocrites when it came to the question of freedom and liberty? How could they *not* have freed their slaves?

One way of understanding Washington is by looking at how many of us live today. Many wealthy and middle-class people accept without much thought that poor people live and suffer in our cities and rural areas. That, too, is part of the world as they find it. Yet, when questioned about it, they agree that there is something wrong about poverty in a country as rich as ours.

If Washington had freed his slaves, he would have created considerable economic hardship for himself. (And by law, he couldn't have freed Martha's slaves.) Besides, he may have weighed the fact that everyone in his social class—wealthy Southerners— was a slave owner.

Only a small minority of Americans owned slaves. How did most Americans feel about slavery?

Many people thought that slavery was part of the natural order of things. They quoted passages from the Bible that seemed to support the idea that God approved of slavery. Others disliked the idea of slavery but didn't care enough to do anything about it. Some people wanted to send slaves back to Africa. A few wanted slavery ended.

The slaves themselves, of course, were against it—not that anybody in power was asking them for their opinion on the matter.

❝ Some view our sable race with scornful eye:
'Their color is a diabolic dye.'
Remember, Christians: Negroes, black as Cain,
May be refined, and join the angelic train. ❞
—From Phillis Wheatley's 1776 poem "On Being Brought from Africa to America," dedicated to George Washington

After leaving the army, did Washington spend all his time at Mount Vernon?

Although retired from the military, Washington was still involved in public life. In 1758 he was elected to the House of Burgesses in Williamsburg, where he helped write the laws that governed the colony. He would serve in the Virginia legislature for more than fifteen years.

Why did Great Britain have an empty purse?

Britain had always looked upon America mostly as a source of revenue. Even in Washington's father's time, Britain's restrictions on American trade had been a source of conflict between home country and colony. By the 1760s and 1770s Parliament had became desperate for funds—Britain had just finished fighting the Seven Years' War, which was long and costly. Furthermore, to protect the

ON THE TABLE AT MOUNT VERNON

Here are just some of the foodstuffs produced at or around Mount Vernon.

Meat: beef, pork, mutton, sausages

Game: deer, rabbits, squirrels, wild turkeys, geese, ducks, turtles

Fish and seafood: lobsters, crabs, oysters, eels, cod, trout, salmon, sturgeon, shad, herring

Vegetables: beans, peas, lentils, squash, pumpkin, sweet potatoes, parsnips, turnips, carrots, leeks, onions, lettuce, cabbages, Jerusalem artichokes

Grains: wheat, corn, barley, rye

Fruits: apples, pears, watermelons, blackberries, strawberries, grapes, persimmons, quinces, peaches

Other: milk, cheese, maple syrup, honey, nuts, pickles and preserves, beer, and cider

Additionally, there would have been imported cane sugar, molasses, wine, rum, tea, coffee, spices, and chocolate as well as limes, lemons, and oranges.

American frontier, it was necessary for Britain to keep a "standing," or permanent, army in the colonies, which was very expensive. And finally, members of Parliament were well aware that the colonists were engaging in a lively smuggling trade with sugar growers in the Caribbean. Products like sugar, molasses, and coffee were being smuggled directly into North America, thereby cutting British sugar growers out of the profits.

To raise money and persuade colonists to buy legally imported sugar and molasses, Parliament passed the Sugar Act in 1764. It was meant to achieve a *monopoly*

> **WHAT DOES IT MEAN?**
>
> A **monopoly** exists when one business or organization controls the production and distribution of a product.

for British sugar growers and to pay for Britain's army in the colonies at the same time.

Why did the colonists hate the Sugar Act?

The Sugar Act contained a crafty idea. The British actually cut the existing tax on molasses so that buying legal, meaning British, molasses was actually cheaper for colonial merchants than buying smuggled goods! So why did the act create such a fuss? The answer is simple: The Sugar Act represented the first time the British Parliament raised money from the colonists without their permission.

Who got to keep the money the Sugar Act raised?

Not the shopkeeper, not the shipper, and not the colonial government. No, the money was meant to support the stationing of regular British troops in the colonies. And the colonists were becoming uneasy. What if the troops were there to do more than protect the frontier? The colonists were unhappy about the new import taxes but paid them.

What was the Stamp Act?

The Stamp Act (1765) taxed the paper used for printed matter of all kinds—newspapers, pamphlets, even playing cards.

Now newspaper readers in the colonies had to pay an extra penny or two just to buy a paper. And people were furious.

The Stamp Act outraged the colonies because it was a direct tax on Americans that had not been passed by their own representatives. As far as they were concerned, only their own general assemblies—not Parliament—had the right to tax colonists. Leading colonists organized a *boycott* that Washington supported. Unless the Stamp Act was *repealed*

> **WHAT DOES IT MEAN?**
> A **boycott** is the refusal to buy, sell, or use a product or service, as a means of protest.

(canceled, or taken back), Americans would refuse to buy British goods. Alarmed, Parliament repealed the Stamp Act after only a year. But at the same time, Parliament declared that it had the right to pass laws, including taxes, for the colonies.

The Stamp Act, even though it was in force for only a year, served to unify the colonies under the cry "No taxation without representation"—meaning that it was unfair for Parliament to tax America when the colonies didn't have the right to vote in the British Parliament.

Did Parliament mean what it said about taxing the colonies?

You bet. The proof was that it passed the Townshend Revenue Act of 1767. Since the colonists had reacted so angrily to a tax paid directly by the consumer (the person buying that newspaper or pamphlet), Parliament decided to levy an *indirect* tax—one that would be paid by the merchants who imported lead, paints, paper, glass, and tea. The consumer would never feel a thing.

But the colonists weren't fooled. They were opposed to any tax, and again they organized a boycott. All the Townshend duties were repealed in 1770—except the one on tea.

When is the last straw like a cup of tea?

The Tea Act, passed by Parliament in 1773, was meant to help Britain's giant East India Company avoid bankruptcy by allowing it exclusive rights to sell tea to the American colonies. By cutting out the middlemen (colonial merchants), the East India Company could pass the savings along to the customer. Tea was now available for less than the smuggled tea that many colonial merchants sold. Of course, when colonists bought the cheaper tea they would also be paying the tax on tea.

The colonists were not fooled. And on top of everything else, the Tea Act angered those merchants in America who often were willing to publicly support Parliament.

❝ The Parliament of Great Britain hath no more right to put their hands into my pocket, without my consent, than I have to put my hands into yours, for money; and this being already urged to them in a firm but decent manner by all the colonies, what reason is there to expect anything from their justice? **❞**

—**Washington** in a 1774 letter, expressing his mounting frustration with Britain's treatment of the colonies

Who was America's last king?

In October 1760 another George was going to help make history. King George III came to the English throne during the Seven Years' War, when he was just twenty-two years old. London-born George III inherited the throne from his grandfather George II. The long war with France, which ended

George III, king of Great Britain and Ireland

in 1763, had left England with huge debts, and the years of fighting had hurt the English economy. Jobs were scarce, crime was high, and there was even rioting in English cities. The English king had plenty of trouble at home without worrying about the upstart American cousins.

But George III's problems were made worse by his own health. In the mid-1760s George III started to show some early signs of going mad. We now know he probably suffered from a disease called *porphyria*, a form of mental illness that is hereditary. Facing a crisis at home and a growing crisis in America, England could have used a king with all his wits.

Who was invited to the Boston Tea Party?

About 150 angry Patriots, cheered on by Samuel Adams and John Hancock. In 1773, angered by the Tea Act, which they believed was designed to force Americans to pay an unfair tax, the men boarded three British ships in Boston Harbor. Dressed as Indians, their faces blackened with burnt cork, the Patriots tossed the ships' cargo— tea—into Boston Harbor.

This was not a little tea. There were more than three hundred chests of tea dumped into the harbor— worth about one million dollars in today's money.

❝ Rally, Mohawks! bring out your axes
And tell King George we'll pay no taxes
On his foreign tea. ❞

—A popular American song

ENLIGHTENING THE ENLIGHTENMENT

The *Enlightenment*, or Age of Reason, was a philosophical movement of the eighteenth century that argued that the universe was rational, that it made sense. Nature wasn't mysterious and frightening, ruled by supernatural, unpredictable forces. Rather, there was a logical order to nature, and this order could be understood through careful, reasoned observation and scientific thinking.

Enlightenment philosophers also believed in the possibility of human progress. People could use their reason to improve themselves and weren't doomed to misery and servitude.

Americans such as Benjamin Franklin, Thomas Jefferson, and Thomas Paine applied Enlightenment ideals to politics. Just as there were laws of nature that governed the universe, people did not have to accept the rule of kings and churches. There was no reason why reasonable people, guided by virtue, couldn't construct a logical and good society in which the people were masters of their own fate—and didn't have to bow before an insane king.

Did Washington attend the Boston Tea Party?

Washington didn't take part in the Boston Tea Party. In fact, he later condemned the action. He felt that the merchants who owned the tea should be paid for the destruction of their property. But he did agree that the English Parliament was acting unfairly and unlawfully.

What was the First Continental Congress?

After the Boston Tea Party, Parliament really cracked down on Massachusetts. Redcoats were sent to march through the streets of Boston. Parliament passed a law shutting down its port. Massachusetts citizens would no longer be allowed to govern themselves at town meetings. "The colonies must either submit or triumph," King George III said.

The colonies would not submit.

In September 1774 representatives from the legislatures of all the colonies except Georgia gathered in Philadelphia. The men—Washington among them—met to discuss what to do about British tyranny. The meeting became known as the First Continental Congress.

"POOR PATSY"

Martha Washington's daughter, Patsy, suffered from the "falling disease," or epilepsy. There was no cure or treatment for the affliction. When Patsy was seventeen, she suffered a massive seizure.

From Washington's diary, June 19, 1773: "At home all day. About five o'clock poor Patsy Custis died suddenly."

Martha was distraught. Though the death of a child or young person was more common in those days, it was still a heavy burden for a mother to bear. George, who also deeply mourned Patsy's death, did what little he could to comfort his wife.

Was Washington the star of the First Continental Congress?

Not really. Washington was not a natural public speaker. Other men, such as the Massachusetts firebrand Samuel Adams, who had plotted the Boston Tea Party, and the outspoken lawyer Patrick Henry of Virginia, were better at rousing a crowd. Reserved, quiet, and dignified, Washington made his presence felt, but in a less flamboyant manner.

AMERICAN VOICES

❝ Is life so dear or peace so sweet as to be purchased at the price of chains and slavery? . . . I know not what course others may take, but as for me, give me liberty or give me death! ❞

—**Patrick Henry,** before the Virginia House of Burgesses, March 1775

Patrick Henry giving his impassioned speech

What did the First Continental Congress do?

Basically, three things:

- It passed a Declaration of Rights. Congress demanded such rights as freedom from taxation without representation, freedom of assembly, and trial by peer.

"No taxation without representation"—there's that famous idea again. Truthfully, the colonists didn't really want representation back in England. A couple of seats in Parliament wouldn't stop the king from doing whatever he liked. What the patriots really wanted was the assurance that they could be taxed only by their own assemblies.

"Freedom of assembly" referred to the right of people to gather together in groups to discuss issues, to organize, to make plans, and to petition the king to *redress* (or fix) their problems.

"Trial by peer" referred to the right of a person charged with a crime to be judged by people similar to himself. In the colonists' case, they wanted Americans to be judged by Americans, not by men living in England. British juries might be quick to condemn Patriots as criminals or traitors.

In short, the First Continental Congress asserted the colonists' right—and, by implication, all people's right—to organize society as they saw fit.

- The Continental Congress also organized a boycott. Starting in December, the colonies would import nothing from Britain. If Britain failed to comply with the colonies' demands by the following September, exports would cease, too.

- Most serious of all, Congress stated that if the Redcoats in Boston were to attack the Patriots there, all the colonies would consider themselves under attack.

The colonies had presented a united front. War was becoming a strong possibility.

The Battle of Lexington

What was "the shot heard round the world"?

In April 1775, Redcoats marched from Boston to the nearby city of Concord to seize Patriot guns and ammunition stored there. The resulting battle—the Battle of Lexington and Concord—left 270 British and 100 or more Americans dead or wounded.

No one knows whether it was a Patriot or a Redcoat who fired the first shot of the war—"the shot heard round the world," as the great American writer Ralph Waldo Emerson would call it in 1837.

Although Washington felt the men who threw the Boston Tea Party had gone too far, when he learned that British soldiers fired upon Americans in Massachusetts, he knew where his loyalties lay— with the colonies. He would support the cause of independence with every ounce of his strength.

The Revolution had begun!

66 Stand your ground. Don't fire unless fired upon, but if they mean to have a war let it begin here! 99
—Attributed to **Commander John Parker** at Lexington

66 Unhappy it is though to reflect, that a brother's sword has been sheathed in a brother's breast, and that the once happy and peaceful plains of America are either to be drenched with blood or inhabited by slaves. Sad alternative! But can a virtuous man hesitate in his choice? 99
—**Washington**, in a May 31, 1775, letter to his old friend George William Fairfax

66 What a glorious morning for America! 99
—**Samuel Adams,** upon hearing the gunfire at Lexington

What did the Continental Congress do?

A month after the Battle of Lexington and Concord, colonial representatives, including Washington, met again in Philadelphia. War was upon them. The Second Continental Congress granted itself the power to raise an army. It named one of its own,

George Washington, commander in chief of the Continental Army. This was a good political choice. Most of the army would come from New England. Washington was a Southerner. With him leading the army, it would show that the colonies were united.

Did Washington lobby hard to get the job of head of the army?

There's no doubt Washington wanted the command. He had attended sessions of Congress in uniform to remind everyone of his military background. He had always been ambitious.

But his ambition was of a peculiarly selfless sort. He refused to accept money for his services, except to cover expenses. His commitment to the cause of liberty was unquestioned. If anyone could be trusted to lead a revolution and not declare himself king, Washington was the man.

Little did anyone—British or American—guess that the war would stretch on for more than eight years of hardship, death, and privation.

AMERICAN VOICES

❝ I this day declare with the utmost sincerity, I do not think myself equal to the command. **❞**
   —**Washington,** upon accepting command of the Continental Army

CHAPTER 4

First in War

The Battle of
Bunker Hill

What was the first thing Washington had to do when he took command of the army?

The first problem was that there was no army.

Before Washington could ride to Boston, colonial and British forces clashed on June 17, 1775, at the Battle of Bunker Hill, outside the city. Arriving in Massachusetts, Washington was appalled to find the ten thousand soldiers untrained, disorderly, and undersupplied. He immediately set to work drilling the men and providing them with uniforms, weapons, and other necessities.

Who won the Battle of Bunker Hill?

Popularly remembered as the Battle of Bunker Hill, most of the fighting actually took place on neighboring Breed's Hill.

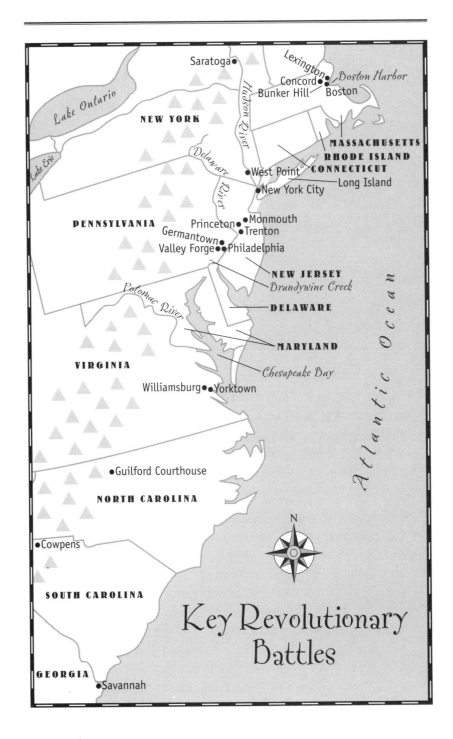

Key Revolutionary
Battles

At first it appeared that the British had won. After all, they took the hill from the Patriot defenders.

Gradually the Patriots realized they had actually scored a victory. The British had lost over one thousand men, including almost one hundred officers, while the Americans had only about four hundred casualties. Redcoats proceeded to occupy Boston, but after losing so many officers they were unable to launch any kind of offensive for nearly a year.

AMERICAN VOICES

❝ Don't one of you fire until you see the whites of their eyes. **❞**

> —**William Prescott**, Patriot leader at Bunker Hill

❝ There they were, the audacious rebels, hard at work making what seemed to me a monstrous fence. . . . At length one who stood conspicuously above the rest waved his bright weapon; the explosion came, attended by the crash of music, the shrieks of the wounded, the groans of the dying. My aunt fainted. . . .

"Oh, how wild and terrific was that long day! . . . Charlestown was in flames; women and children flying from their burning houses sought refuge in the city. Dismay and terror, wailing and distraction impressed their picture on my memory, never to be effaced. . . . I have read many times of the glory of war, but this one battle taught me, however it be painted by poet or novelist, there is nothing but woe and sorrow and shame to be found in the reality. **❞**

> —**Dorothea Gamsby**, who was ten years old when she witnessed the Battle of Bunker Hill from the attic window of her Loyalist family's house in Charlestown, a Boston neighborhood

REVOLUTIONARY WAR ARTILLERY

There were three basic types of *artillery*, or cannons: guns, howitzers, and mortars.

Guns were what we nowadays commonly think of as cannons. They had long, narrow barrels and were relatively lightweight. They fired low to the ground and were fairly accurate. Guns could fire solid cannonballs, exploding bombs, or *scattershot*—loose fragments that sprayed over an area. They were best used against troops on the battlefield.

Howitzers were aimed lower than mortars but higher than guns. Able to fire the heaviest balls and bombs, howitzers were used to smash down the walls and embankments of forts.

Mortars were short and squat and fired projectiles high into the air. They were often used to heave bombs over the walls of forts. The bombs were designed to explode in midair, raining shrapnel down on the enemy.

How did Washington's first campaign of the war go?

Though the British held Boston, Patriots occupied the hills surrounding the city. But without enough cannons, Washington could not rain bombs on the British forces in the city and in the harbor. All was not lost, though. In the winter of 1775–1776, cannons were captured from the British at Fort Ticonderoga in upstate New York and brought to Boston. Washington quickly set them up on the high ground overlooking the city. With the rebel cannons aimed at them, the British loaded up the troops and sailed out of Boston in March 1776.

The British had left the thirteen colonies—
temporarily. Washington knew they would be back.

What did the Declaration of Independence declare?

In Philadelphia on July 4, 1776, the Continental
Congress issued the Declaration of Independence,
which basically stated that the American colonies
no longer considered themselves to be a part of the
British Empire. Written by Thomas Jefferson of
Virginia, the Declaration was signed by the fifty-six
members of Congress who were able to attend the
session in which it was adopted. Washington, in
Massachusetts rallying the army, did not sign.

John Hancock of Massachusetts was the first to sign
the Declaration of Independence. Legend has it that
he wrote his name extra large so that the king could
read it without having to put on his spectacles.
Today, to "put your John Hancock" on something
means to sign it.

Hancock's large signature was a show of bravado.
Let's not forget that, to the British authorities,
Congress was an illegal, treasonous body and its
members were traitors. There would be harsh
consequences if the revolution failed, and the
Patriots knew it. After Hancock signed, he said, "We
must all hang together," meaning everyone should

AMERICAN VOICES

❝ We hold these truths to be self-evident; that all men
are created equal; that they are endowed by their
creator with certain unalienable rights; that among
these are life, liberty, and the pursuit of happiness. ❞
—**Thomas Jefferson,** Declaration of Independence, 1776

sign. But Benjamin Franklin famously said, after adding his name to the list of "traitors," "Yes. We must all hang together. Or assuredly we shall all hang separately."

AMERICAN VOICES

❝ Society in every state is a blessing, but Government, even in its best state, is but a necessary evil; in its worst state, an intolerable one. **❞**
—**Thomas Paine,** in the widely read pamphlet *Common Sense* (1776), arguing that British domination over America must end

❝ Innumerable are the advantages of our connection with Britain; and a just dependence on her is a sure way to avoid the horrors and calamities of war. **❞**
—Maryland Loyalist **James Chalmers** in *Plain Truth*, his 1776 rebuttal to Paine's *Common Sense*. Not all Americans supported the revolutionaries.

How did Washington narrowly escape disaster in New York?

Washington knew that Britain's next logical point of attack would be New York City. The second-largest city in the colonies (after Philadelphia), with an excellent port, it was also located about midway down the American coastline. Losing New York would split the thirteen colonies in two.

Collecting about 27,000 men, Washington set up defenses on Long Island, Manhattan Island, and the mainland in New Jersey. Strung out in a narrow chain, the army was vulnerable to attack at any number of points.

In August 1776, more than 35,000 British and Hessian troops descended on the area. Thousands of Patriots on Long Island were ferried across the East River to Manhattan in the middle of the night. They had been lucky to escape capture, though they were still in danger of being surrounded.

New York was a different place then, of course. There were farms where there are now tall buildings. Washington led his troops gallantly, even recklessly. But the poorly trained, inexperienced rebel soldiers were no match for the mighty British attackers. Washington was forced to retreat. From Manhattan he led his army across New Jersey and into Pennsylvania, where it could regroup. Washington had ceded New York City to the British, but he had avoided disaster. And he had shown he would not allow the war to end quickly.

The British army would have followed and possibly finished Washington in New York if not for a mysterious fire. It started on September 21, near the future site of the World Trade Center. Driven by a wind, the great fire destroyed nearly five hundred buildings, almost one-fifth of old New York.

There are legends about who started the fire, including a story that it was the work of a young woman who wanted to help Washington's army. No one knows for sure who started the fire, but the British arrested anyone they thought was suspicious. One of those arrested was a man who said he was a schoolteacher but later confessed to the British that he was a spy for George Washington. General Howe, the British commander, ordered his execution. His name was Nathan Hale.

Musket or Rifle?

First, what's the difference? A *musket* (shown below) was a long, smoothbore gun that fired a round lead ball. A *rifle* was a long gun that had spiral grooves on the inside of the barrel. The grooves put a spin on the bullet the rifle fired. Rifles were much more accurate than muskets.

The Revolutionary War was fought on both sides mostly with muskets. Though more accurate, rifles took far longer to reload. Also, they could not be equipped with bayonets.

Because they were so inaccurate, muskets were useless beyond about one hundred yards. Opposing *infantry* (foot soldiers) had to approach to about that distance. Each side would then fire, rush forward, fire again, rush forward, and so on, until engaged in hand-to-hand combat with bayonets and knives. A skilled musketeer could fire a shot once every fifteen seconds—quick enough for two, possibly three, rounds before having to resort to the bayonet.

Rifles were used mainly by sharpshooters to protect the *flanks* (sides) of a mass of infantry, or for other specialized purposes.

❝I only regret that I have but one life to lose for my country.❞

—Nathan Hale's legendary last words. He was hanged on September 22, 1776, on what is now New York City's Third Avenue and Sixty-fifth Street.

Where did Washington celebrate Christmas in 1776?

By late December 1776, winter weather had halted the fighting. The British had set up camp in the New Jersey towns of Bordentown and Trenton. There they planned to sit out the winter and wait for the fighting to resume in the spring.

Across the Delaware River, in Pennsylvania, Washington was growing desperate. He had lost New York City. Many of his men were due to be sent home at the end of the year. He needed some sort of victory, if only a symbolic one.

WHAT THE HECK WAS A HESSIAN?

Hessians were German soldiers who were paid to fight for Britain. They weren't *mercenaries*—individuals willing to fight for anyone who would pay them—in the classic sense. Rather, they were units sent by their German rulers to serve under British command. Britain paid various German princes for the use of Hessian soldiers.

On Christmas night Washington led 2,400 soldiers across the icy Delaware. Arriving in Trenton at daybreak, the Patriots took 1,500 Hessians by surprise, killing about 30 and capturing 900. None of Washington's men was killed.

Rashly, Washington marched deeper into New Jersey, meeting the British on January 3 at Princeton.

The battle was going poorly for the Patriots until Washington himself rode to the front of the lines, urging his men on. The Patriots rallied and won the battle. The score: 273 British killed or captured, only 40 Patriots killed or wounded.

Exhausted, hungry, and in danger of being surrounded, Washington's army marched north to the safety of the New Jersey hill country. There they rested, basked in the success of the winter campaign, and waited for spring.

"WASHINGTON CROSSING THE DELAWARE"

In the famous 1851 painting of Washington crossing the Delaware, only two figures besides Washington have been positively identified. One is future president James Monroe, shown holding the flag. The other is an African-American oarsman named Prince Whipple. Born in Africa, Whipple was sent by his parents to America to be educated. Instead he was sold into slavery by the captain of the ship that brought him over. Whipple accompanied his owner, a New Hampshire merchant and signer of the Declaration of Independence named William Whipple, on Washington's Trenton campaign.

The British held New York City. What was their next target?

Philadelphia. As the winter of 1776–1777 ended, Washington tried to figure out where the British, from their base in New York, would strike next. Would they move north up the Hudson River, to meet British armies coming down from Canada? Or would they move south, toward Philadelphia? Through the spring and summer, Washington waited.

Finally, in August 1777, he got his answer. A fleet of more than 250 British ships carrying at least 15,000 soldiers had been spotted in Delaware Bay. Patriot forts prevented the fleet from moving up the Delaware River to Philadelphia. Instead, the fleet sailed south and then north, up the unguarded Chesapeake Bay to its northern end. Washington knew the British were planning to march the short distance overland to Philadelphia.

LET LOOSE THE DOGS OF WAR?

After Germantown, the Americans discovered they had taken an unusual prisoner—the opposing general's dog. Ever the gentleman, Washington returned the unfortunate canine to the British commander, General Sir William Howe, along with the following note:

"General Washington's compliments to General Howe. He does himself the pleasure to return him a dog, which accidentally fell into his hands, and by the inscription on the collar appears to belong to General Howe."

Washington raced through Philadelphia and met the British at Brandywine Creek, outside the city. Badly outnumbered, the Patriots lost the battle. The British took Philadelphia, the capital city, with little further resistance. Congress had fled only days before, to nearby York, Pennsylvania.

In October Washington attacked British forces camped in Germantown, outside Philadelphia. Fog contributed to the confusion of the disorderly attack, and the colonials were forced to retreat.

A STAR-SPANGLED WHOPPER?

Didn't Betsy Ross sew the first American flag?

Possibly.

Long after she was dead, one of Ross's grandsons wrote a book claiming that, in May 1776, Washington and two members of Congress came to Ross and asked her to sew a flag based on a rough sketch they had drawn. According to the story, Ross suggested five-pointed stars rather than six-pointed stars, sewed the flag, and the rest is history.

Did it happen that way? Maybe. Betsy Ross did work as a seamstress in Philadelphia, and it's known that she sewed flags. But there is no mention in the congressional records or by Washington of the famous meeting. Many historians now doubt the truth of the tale.

But it's a nice story—and it might even be true.

Whether or not Betsy Ross sewed the first flag in 1776, a year later Congress officially adopted the design on June 14, 1777. "Resolved: That the flag of the thirteen United States be thirteen stripes alternate red and white; that the Union be thirteen stars, white in a blue field, representing a new constellation."

Was Washington the only general in the Continental Army?

As commander in chief, Washington spent most of the war in the area of New York and Philadelphia, the most important cities in America. But the war was being fought in many other places: upstate New York and New England, the West, the Tidewater Virginia area, the Carolinas, Georgia. Here are some other important Continental Army commanders:

• Major General Horatio Gates led American forces in the north to important early victories over the British in Vermont and in the Hudson River Valley. Gates was so successful, in fact, that there were calls in Congress to have him replace Washington as head of the army. Gates fell out of favor later when he was assigned to fight in the South and suffered lopsided defeats.

• Expert in the use of artillery, Major General Henry Knox, known as "Ox" because of his size, led the 1775 bombardment of Boston. Under Washington, Knox commanded the artillery at numerous battles, including Trenton, Brandywine, and the final siege of the war, Yorktown. Knox and Washington became lifelong friends.

- On the western frontier (what is now Indiana and Illinois), Lieutenant Colonel George Rogers Clark defended colonial settlements from raids by Native Americans and their British supporters. Clark's younger brother, William, would later gain fame under President Jefferson as co-leader of the Lewis and Clark overland expedition to the Pacific.

- General Nathanael Greene was perhaps the best military mind of the Revolutionary War. Rising from the rank of private in the Rhode Island militia to become a trusted adviser of Washington at Trenton and Brandywine, Greene eventually was appointed commander of the southern forces. He scored important victories over the British at Cowpens in South Carolina and at the Guilford Courthouse in North Carolina.

- Daring, brave, and ambitious, General Benedict Arnold took part in many key northern battles during the early part of the war. He was wounded twice and nearly died on several occasions. Washington placed great trust in him and named him commander of the army headquarters at West Point in New York. (We'll hear more about Benedict Arnold later on.)

Three non-Americans became important military leaders for the Continentals:

- Having served in the Prussian army during the Seven Years' War, Baron Friedrich von Steuben was expert in European methods of drill and maneuvers. Not knowing English, von Steuben tried yelling at the disorganized Americans in German. When it became clear that the men couldn't understand his orders, he took to swearing at them in French with a captain who spoke that language translating his curses into English. Despite his unconventional methods, he was successful in improving discipline in the Continental ranks.

- A young French nobleman, the Marquis de Lafayette, was not twenty years old when he volunteered to serve in the Continental Army; he became one of Washington's most trusted commanders as well as his close personal friend. After the American Revolution ended, Lafayette returned to Europe, where he supported the cause of republicans in the French Revolution.

- Finally, Thaddeus Kościuszko, a Polish aristocrat and military engineer, used his skills to design fortifications that proved critical in winning the war.

In the fall of 1777, the British held New York and Philadelphia. Why didn't the Patriots give up the fight?

For one thing, most colonists did not live in cities. So although they'd been forced to surrender Philadelphia and New York, the Continental Army was intact. It had suffered no disastrous defeats. Against superior numbers, Washington had coordinated strategic retreats. And in October, Continentals under General Horatio Gates scored a huge victory in upstate New York at the Battle of Saratoga. About 5,700 Redcoats and Hessians were taken prisoner. The victory at Saratoga didn't win the war. But it did win America an important new friend.

That friend was France.

CHAPTER 5

Posterity Will Huzzah for Us

Washington and his troops at Valley Forge

Who came into the war on the side of the colonies?

For months Benjamin Franklin had been in Paris, trying to convince the French to come to the aid of the Patriots. The problem was, he had nothing to offer France in exchange for its help in the war . . . except one thing: If America won its independence, Britain would be weakened and humiliated.

It turned out to be enough. France supported America not because it wanted to promote liberty (France was ruled by a king), but to punish its old enemy, Britain.

Why did America need France's help?

- America had virtually no navy. British warships could blockade American cities with impunity. French ships would go a long way in neutralizing British naval superiority.

- Even though much of it was an ocean away, Britain's army was far larger than America's. French soldiers could help even the odds.

- America was having trouble supplying the soldiers it could muster. French clothing, blankets, guns, gunpowder, and, most importantly, French money could keep Patriots fighting longer.

NOBLE SAVAGES?

Many influential Frenchmen were followers of the ideas of the philosopher Jean-Jacques Rousseau (1712–1778). Rousseau believed that civilization served only to make people unhappy. To Rousseau the "noble savage" who lived in a state of nature, without the trappings of civilization, was better off than a pampered English lord.

Although Indians were viewed as the ideal "noble savages," the French viewed Americans—who seemed to live in a land free of the corrupting influences of centuries of civilization—as noble savages as well. It was a romantic and hardly accurate view. But it was one that Benjamin Franklin promoted in order to win public sympathy for America's cause.

What do armies do in winter?

Washington's army spent the next six months encamped at Valley Forge, Pennsylvania. In those days armies didn't fight during the winter months, because snow, ice, and freezing temperatures made troop movements impractical.

The winter of 1777–1778 was brutally harsh. There wasn't enough food. Blankets and coats were scarce. Many of the troops no longer had shoes. Disease was common, and hundreds of men died.

It was all Washington could do to keep the men from deserting. A strict disciplinarian, the general was not above the use of force to put down rebellion in the ranks, and he had more than one deserter shot. Despite the hardships, however, morale improved as winter turned to spring. The system of supplying the troops was improved. Word came that the French were entering the war. Through his interpreter, Baron von Steuben drilled and exercised the men, and General Knox helped erect defenses to protect the troops. By the time the army broke camp, in June, the soldiers were better prepared than they had ever been.

AMERICAN VOICES

66 For some days past there has been little less than a famine in camp. A part of the army has been a week without any kind of flesh, and the rest for three or four days. Naked and starving as they are, we cannot enough admire the incomparable patience and fidelity of the soldiery, that they have not been ere this excited by their sufferings to a general mutiny or dispersion. **99**

—**Washington**, in a letter to New York governor George Clinton asking for help at Valley Forge, winter 1778

Who was with Washington at Valley Forge?

Martha Washington. She visited George every winter during the war, while fighting was suspended.

Though George and Martha did not marry for what we would call "romantic love," over the years they grew genuinely fond of each other. Their respect and admiration was mutual, and each treated the other with loyalty and generosity.

❝I am only fond of what comes from the heart. . . . I know too much of the vanity of human affairs to expect felicity from the splendid scenes of public life. I am still determined to be cheerful and happy, in whatever situation I may be; for I have also learned from experience that the greater part of our happiness or misery depends upon our dispositions, and not upon our circumstances. We carry the seeds of the one or the other about with us, in our minds, wherever we go.❞

—**Martha Washington,** in a letter to Mercy Otis Warren

Who was Molly Pitcher?

In June 1778 the British army, fearing it would be trapped by the French fleet in Philadelphia, abandoned the city. As the British were marching across New Jersey to New York City, Washington ordered an attack. The armies clashed near the town of Monmouth, New Jersey.

During the battle, a woman named Mary Hays fetched water for her husband and his fellow artillerymen. The water cooled the men and their cannons, and Hays earned the nickname "Molly Pitcher" for her efforts. Legend has it that when her husband fell wounded, she assumed his place at the cannon. For this she also became known as "Sergeant Molly."

The Battle of Monmouth ended more or less in a draw. The British continued on to New York City, with Washington and his army trailing behind.

Revolutionary Uniform

There was a wide variation in uniform types in the Continental Army. This was true for British soldiers, too—soldiers on both sides sometimes wore green coats.

A typical well-equipped American infantryman might have had:

Leather cap with bearskin crest, red-and-black feather plume

Blue coat with white trim

Buff-colored waistcoat

Buff-colored breeches

Stockings

Buckled black leather shoes

Musket with bayonet

Canteen

Cartridge box for carrying powder and shot

Red knapsack for carrying blanket, tinderbox, pipe, money, map, folding knife and fork, fishhook and sinkers, sundial-compass, dice, paper and pen, hunting knife, needle and thread, scissors, and other items

Who fought in the Continental Army?

Most of the men in the Continental Army were untrained farmers, laborers, and other common folk, ranging from middle-aged graybeards to boys as young as nine. Many hardly knew how to care for a gun properly, let alone shoot one. They joined up for a number of reasons: promises made by Congress or the states of money or land in payment, dreams of heroism and glory, or simple patriotism. About one in twelve soldiers was African American, though the British did their best to lure away slaves by promising freedom to any African American who crossed ranks.

Who were "camp followers"?

The hordes of people, necessary and otherwise, who accompanied an army in its travels were known as camp followers. These included wives and families of the soldiers, as well as *sutlers* (food suppliers), doctors, craftsmen, wagoneers, postal riders, spies, musicians, the press, and others. Many camp followers were women, who often received *half-rations* (food and shelter) from the army in return for their service as nurses, cooks, laundresses, or general laborers.

What did Washington do during 1779 and 1780?

Not much, at least in the way of actual fighting. The British army occupied New York City. Washington's army camped outside the city. Neither side could do much about the other. The two opponents were locked in a stalemate.

Meanwhile, the war raged elsewhere. In 1779 British naval forces attacked ports in the southern states, capturing Savannah, Georgia, and occupying Portsmouth and Norfolk, Virginia, both of which had already been burned to the ground in the spring of 1776.

In the spring of 1780, the British captured Charleston, South Carolina, along with 5,500 American soldiers under the command of General

Benjamin Lincoln of Massachusetts. It was the single worst defeat of the war for the Patriots. In the north, French warships arrived in New England but were unable to put much of a dent in British positions at Newport, Rhode Island.

From his base in New Jersey, Washington spent much of his energy in trying to wrest more and better supplies out of Congress. For two years he played a waiting game—trying to avoid defeat, hoping the tide of war would turn. In 1781 it would.

❝ Gentlemen: In [a previous letter] I barely expressed our want of shoes. I did not then know the extent of our wants, or that there was not a single pair in the hands of the clothier at camp to supply them. **❞**
—**Washington**, in a 1780 letter to Congress, complaining about the lack of supplies

What is a "Benedict Arnold"?

A bold and daring Patriot leader in the early days of the Revolution, General Benedict Arnold was also greedy, ambitious, and ruthless. Crippled from wounds, caught up in shady business dealings, and embittered by promotions that came too slowly, by the summer of 1780 Arnold had turned traitor. He plotted to hand over army headquarters at West Point, New York, to the British.

When Arnold's British contact, Major John André, was captured with the plans in his boots, Arnold fled to a British ship. André was hanged as a spy. Arnold went on to command British forces in New

England and Virginia. He was as skillful a leader of British troops as he had been of Americans.

Washington and his staff were shaken by the act of high treason, but Arnold had caused little real damage, and the American side soon recovered.

Today, any traitor can be called a "Benedict Arnold."

❝ . . . from the known humanity of your Excellence I am induced to ask your protection for Mrs. Arnold from every insult and injury that the mistaken vengeance of my country may expose her to. It ought to fall only on me. She is as good and as innocent as an angel, and is incapable of doing wrong. **❞**

—**Benedict Arnold,** writing to Washington soon after fleeing West Point, asking him to show mercy to his young Loyalist bride, Margaret Shippen Arnold. Unaware that Mrs. Arnold had in fact been involved in the plot, Washington made sure that she was able to rejoin her husband.

What happened at Yorktown?

At the end of May 1781, a large British army—about 8,000 troops—gathered in Virginia under the command of General Charles Lord Cornwallis. During the spring and early summer, Redcoat forces raided towns and supply stations throughout Virginia. Washington prepared to march south out of New Jersey and confront the British.

The Patriots were victorious. The last major battle of the war was over. Scattered fighting continued, but the end was near.

The World Turned Upside Down?

It's said that during the official ceremony marking Cornwallis's surrender, the British military band played a popular tune called "The World Turned Upside Down."

Well, it's possible. It's also possible the band played the tune but had in mind the alternative lyrics: "When the King Enjoys His Own Again."

From "The World Turned Upside Down":
If buttercups buzzed after the bee,
If boats were on land, churches on sea . . .
If summer were spring and the other way round,
Then all the world would be upside down.

From "When the King Enjoys His Own Again":
My skill goes beyond the depths of a pond
Or river in the greatest rain
Whereby I tell all things will be well
When the King enjoys his own again.

In response, the Continental military band played "Yankee Doodle"—a song the British had once sung to mock the colonists' supposedly unsophisticated manners, but which the Americans had adopted as an anthem of pride.

Then Washington learned that a large French fle thirty warships—was heading toward the Chesapeake.

Quickly collecting about 8,800 Patriots, plus anot 7,800 French troops who had marched from New England, he began moving his army south. He ho to trap Cornwallis between his own army and th advancing French warships.

As if fulfilling Washington's greatest hopes, the French fleet defeated the British fleet at the mou of the Chesapeake. Cornwallis's army could no longer escape by ship. It was stuck in Yorktown, Virginia. Though Cornwallis had built fortificatior around the town, the position was impossible to defend.

For three weeks Washington's American and Fren troops bombarded the Redcoats. Finally, on Octob 17, a drummer boy emerged from the British cam and approached Washington's forces. The gunner: held their fire. Behind the drummer boy appeared British officer holding up a white handkerchief. Cornwallis's army had surrendered.

Two days later, on October 19, the British soldiers marched out of Yorktown and gave up their arms. Too proud—or perhaps too humiliated—to surrenc in person, Cornwallis sent his second-in-command, General Charles O'Hara, to the ceremony. In respons Washington gave his second, General Benjamin Lincoln (who had suffered the terrible defeat at Charleston the year before), the honor of accepting O'Hara's sword.

Why did a single defeat spell the end of the British war effort?

The defeat at Yorktown wasn't crippling to the British from a purely military standpoint. After all, Cornwallis had lost "only" about 8,000 men, and there were plenty more soldiers where they came from.

> ### A CLASSY GUY
>
> After Yorktown, Washington asked his troops not to humiliate the defeated Redcoats by jeering at them. "Posterity will huzzah for us," he assured his men.

For England's leaders, however, the loss at Yorktown was a crushing defeat. The war had been popular in England in 1776. But five years of fighting had sapped the nation's enthusiasm for bloodshed. Many Britishers felt the American conflict was King George's war and none of their affair. Now the nation had been humiliated in battle. How long, the people asked, must this pointless war go on? Clearly the Americans intended to keep fighting as long as it took.

After Yorktown the British would grant the former colonies their independence.

Why did Washington's happiness over the victory at Yorktown not last long?

Shortly after the siege of Yorktown ended, Washington learned that Jack Custis, Martha's son and George's stepson, had contracted "camp fever" (typhus) and was at the home in Eltham, Virginia, of one of Washington's good friends. The commander in chief rode there as fast as he could. Sadly, his stepson died on November 5, 1781, leaving four children. George and Martha were now childless, though they eventually adopted Jack's two youngest children as their own.

What was the Treaty of Paris?

Communications were slow in those days. You couldn't just pick up the phone and call London. Messages had to be relayed across the ocean by ship. Also, the British were engaged in conflicts in other parts of the world, which often took up Parliament's time and attention.

So it wasn't until September 1783 that Britain, France, and the United States agreed on a final treaty. Called the Treaty of Paris for the city where it was signed, the agreement called for British recognition of American independence.

What did France receive in return for its critical aid to America? Not much, other than the pleasure of seeing Britain brought low.

He'd won the war. What was next for Washington?

Washington was a hero to the people. He was respected by local and national political leaders. He had won the absolute loyalty of his officers and thus control of the army.

With the ouster of the British, there was no central authority to govern the land. Congress was weak—it didn't even have the power to collect taxes unless all thirteen states agreed. The war-hardened army, completely loyal to its seemingly invincible commander in chief, could easily brush aside the likes of Jefferson and Adams—men who served the nation in several ways but never in combat. And the very popular Benjamin Franklin was considered too old to serve.

The next step was obvious: Washington would declare himself king for life. The army would install him in Philadelphia as such.

And that's why today the United States is a hereditary monarchy ruled by descendants of Martha Custis Washington!

Ummm . . . it didn't turn out that way, did it?

Contrary to many people's expectations, Washington fulfilled the trust Congress had put in him. He walked away from power, resigning his military commission late in 1783.

What happened at Fraunces Tavern?

On December 4, 1783, Washington said farewell to his senior officers at Fraunces Tavern in New York City. Colonel Benjamin Talmadge was among those present:

Such a scene of sorrow and weeping I had never before witnessed, and hope I may never be called upon to witness again. . . . The simple thought that we were then about to part from the man who had conducted us through a long and bloody war, and under whose conduct the glory and independence of our country had been achieved, and that we should see his face no more in this world, seemed to me utterly insupportable.

What did Washington say in bidding farewell to Congress?

After saying good-bye to his officers, Washington rode to Annapolis, Maryland, where Congress was in session, to submit his resignation from the army. In a brief address, Washington stated: "I consider it an indispensable duty to close this last solemn act of my official life, by commending the interests of our dearest country to the protection of Almighty God, and those who have the superintendence of them, to his holy keeping."

Taking leave of Congress, Washington set out for Mount Vernon and arrived there on Christmas Eve. He had returned to the comfort of home once again.

VOICES FROM HISTORY

" If this is true, he is the greatest man in history. **"**
—**George III,** supposedly, on hearing that Washington had refused to seize power for himself

CHAPTER 6

First in Peace

Washington watches the signing of the Constitution.

The United States had won its independence. What now?

In 1777 Congress had drawn up the Articles of Confederation—an agreement among the states on how the country was to be run, now that the king and Parliament were no longer in charge. Not *ratified* (accepted) by the states until 1781, the Articles outlined Congress's powers, which were extremely limited. Under the Articles, there was neither an executive (presidential) branch nor a judicial (courts) branch of government.

Basically the central government didn't exist. To many people, including Washington, it was clear that if the United States was going to survive as one nation, a stronger government was needed.

The way to form a stronger central government? Replace the Articles of Confederation with something else—a new *constitution.*

NOT ENOUGH POWER?

According to the Articles of Confederation, Congress could:

- make treaties with foreign nations

- administer the territories of the U.S. beyond the Appalachian Mountains

- raise an army or navy

- and not much else

Among the things Congress could not do were:

- impose taxes (Congress could only ask the states for money)

- make citizens or states do what it wanted (state law overruled national law)

- regulate interstate commerce or foreign trade

What was the Constitutional Convention?

The Constitutional Convention was a meeting held in Philadelphia in 1787 by representatives of all the states except Rhode Island. Their task was to figure out how the new nation would govern itself and to write down the rules in a new constitution.

The problems were many: How to balance the interests of small states and large states? North and South? Rich citizen and poor? Most critical of all, the states had just fought a war to rid themselves of an oppressive power. How could they balance the need for a strong *federal* (central) government with the rights of states and individuals?

Washington was the obvious choice to preside over the convention. Respected and trusted by all and viewed as a moderate, he would be willing to listen to opposing sides.

It was a lively, often contentious meeting. In the end, after four months' work, the convention produced the Constitution that still forms the fundamental basis of our government.

AMERICAN VOICES

❝ A few short weeks will determine the political fate of America for the present generation and probably produce no small influence on the happiness of society through a long succession of ages to come. ❞
—**Washington**, in a letter to his old friend the Marquis de Lafayette, during the Constitutional Convention

What are checks and balances?

In large part written by Washington's fellow Virginian James Madison, the Constitution relies on a system of checks and balances to ensure that no part of government becomes too powerful. It provides for three branches of government:

- the legislative (Congress)
- the executive (headed by the president)
- the judicial (the courts)

Each branch has certain powers, or checks, over the other two; in this way they balance each other out.

For instance, only the legislature can write new laws. But the president can refuse to put them into effect by vetoing them, and the Supreme Court can declare them unconstitutional (illegal).

66 We the people of the United States, in order to form a more perfect Union, establish justice, insure domestic tranquility, provide for the common defense, promote the general welfare, and secure the blessings of liberty to ourselves and our posterity do ordain and establish this Constitution for the United States of America. 99

—from the Constitution

66 Be assured his influence carried this government. 99
—**James Monroe,** writing to Jefferson of Washington's impact on the debate surrounding the ratification of the Constitution

How did Washington come to be the first president?

Congress arranged to have the Electoral College meet in March 1789 to elect the president. It was obvious to everyone that Washington, the hero of the Revolution, would be chosen the first president.

The Electoral College

Nowadays the electoral college is rarely in the news. (A lot of Americans had never heard of the electoral college before the disputed 2000 election between Al Gore and George W. Bush.) Technically, the electoral college still elects the president. But in practice it merely makes official what the voting public has already decided.

When the Constitution was written, the Framers had little trust in the wisdom of the citizenry. They feared that, left to their own devices, the people might one day elect a semiliterate buffoon— or worse. The Framers also wanted to design a system whereby the president would have to win broad support from many areas of the country, rather than overwhelming support from a single area. So the Framers placed a step between the people and the president— the electoral college.

The members of the electoral college (who would themselves be chosen by the states, using a variety of methods) would elect the president. The Framers hoped that the electors would be wiser and more objective than the citizenry. Ideally the electors would simply choose the best man for the job.

The system worked as planned in the first two presidential elections. There were no political parties yet, and Washington was clearly the best man for the job. The electoral college had no problem in choosing him. By the time Washington retired, however, the first political parties—the Federalists and the Republicans—had come along and taken over national politics. Members of the electoral college were selected on the basis of their loyalty to one party or the other. Choosing the best man was no longer the electors' primary objective; choosing their party's man was. It's been that way ever since.

Did Washington run for president?

No. On the contrary, he agreed to serve as president somewhat unwillingly. After years of public service in Virginia's House of Burgesses, Congress, and in the military, fifty-seven-year-old Washington wanted nothing more than to return to the peace of Mount Vernon. But he recognized the new nation's need for a unifying figure, and he knew that only he could fill the role. He had always had an overpowering sense of duty. And it was his duty to serve when called.

On April 30, 1789, in New York City, he was sworn in as president.

AMERICAN VOICES

❝ He has a dignity which forbids familiarity mixed with an easy affability which creates love and reverence. **❞**

—**Abigail Adams,** wife of John Adams, describing Washington

It's been said that Washington was elected unanimously. Does that mean every single person in the whole country voted for him?

No. First, very few people could vote back then. The rules varied from state to state, but most states barred women, slaves, and those without land from voting. . . . So there were plenty of people who, even if they had wanted to, couldn't have voted for Washington.

Second, the president wasn't elected by the people directly. It was the electoral college that voted unanimously for Washington. John Adams, of Massachusetts, was elected vice president.

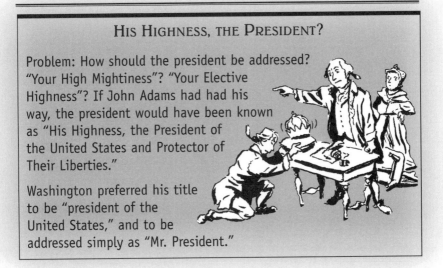

Did Washington store his socks in the presidential cabinet?

Of course not. The *cabinet* was a small circle of Washington's most trusted advisers, each of whom headed a department of government. It was Washington, in fact, who created the institution of the presidential cabinet. Today the presidential cabinet consists of about a dozen members. Washington's cabinet included only four: the secretary of war, the secretary of state, the secretary of the treasury, and the attorney general.

Who were the "Big Two" of Washington's administration?

Alexander Hamilton and Thomas Jefferson.

Hamilton and Jefferson represented conflicting ideas about what government could do and what America should be.

Hamilton, along with James Madison and John Jay, had written a series of essays called *The Federalist*

Papers. The Federalists argued for a strong federal government that would further the interests of those who had the most stake in society—the wealthy. Hamilton feared the "rabble," lower social and economic classes. His America was populated by bankers, lawyers, and rich planters and manufacturers.

Jefferson was leader of the Anti-Federalists, also known as the Republicans. He saw the federal government as a threat to individual liberty.

GEORGE WASHINGTON, THE EIGHTH PRESIDENT?

Was Washington really the *eighth* president of the United States?

In a sense, yes.

Remember that Congress had declared independence from Britain in 1776 and drawn up the Articles of Confederation in 1777. The states ratified the Articles in March 1781, six months before Yorktown.

Under the rules of the Articles of Confederation, on November 5, 1781, John Hanson of Maryland was chosen to *preside* over, or lead, Congress—making him the first president of the new nation! Since there was no separate executive branch of government, Hanson's role as president of Congress can be compared to that of today's Speaker of the House. Nevertheless, Hanson served as president until November 3, 1782. Six other men also served one-year terms as president under the Articles of Confederation:

John Hanson (1781–82)
Elias Boudinot (1783–84)
Thomas Mifflin (1784–85)
Richard Henry Lee (1785–86)

Nathan Gorman (1786–87)
Arthur St. Clair (1787–88)
Cyrus Griffin (1788–89)

George Washington was the first president to serve a four-year term under the Constitution and head up the executive branch. But you could argue he was actually the eighth president.

Government was a necessary evil—the less it did, the better. His America was populated by independent farmers, virtuous laborers, and honest tradesmen.

Washington had sympathy for both Federalist and Republican points of view. He recognized that both Hamilton and Jefferson were brilliant thinkers. And so he appointed both men to his first cabinet. Hamilton served as secretary of the treasury and Jefferson as secretary of state. Washington spent much of his first term trying to make peace between his two warring advisers.

Sec'y Treasury   Sec'y State

Why did the capital move from New York City to Philadelphia and then to its permanent location on the banks of the Potomac River?

Alexander Hamilton wanted the federal government to pay off certain debts that the states had taken on during the Revolutionary War. Jefferson opposed the idea on the grounds that doing so would only make the states more dependent on the federal government. Besides, some of the southern states had already paid off their debt. What was in it for them?

> ### TEENY TINY GOVERNMENT
>
> More people worked for Washington at Mount Vernon than worked for him in the executive branch of the federal government.

Hamilton suggested a deal. He knew that Jefferson, a Virginian, wanted the capital in a southerly location.

Money in the Bank

During Washington's first term, Republicans and Federalists argued over the wisdom of creating a National Bank to be run as a business by the government.

Republicans wanted the government to remain as small as possible. They opposed the bank, on the grounds that running a bank wasn't part of the government's job according to the Constitution.

Federalists wanted to expand the government. They supported the bank, arguing that the government had the right to do lots of things not mentioned specifically by the Constitution.

In 1791 the president asked both Jefferson and Hamilton to submit to him their views on the matter.

Jefferson: "To take a single step beyond the boundaries . . . specifically drawn [by the Constitution] around the powers of Congress is to take possession of a boundless field of power."

Hamilton: "It is not denied that there are implied as well as express powers."

Not totally convinced by either side, Washington deferred to Hamilton, since he was secretary of the treasury, and signed the bank into law later that year. The bank was dissolved in 1811, but the idea that the Constitution granted "implied powers" to the government has held ever since.

If southern states would support the federal assumption of debt, northern states would agree to move the capital south, first to Philadelphia and then to the banks of the Potomac River.

Jefferson agreed. It took about ten years to lay out streets, erect buildings, and otherwise prepare the swampy site. In 1800 the government moved to the new federal city, by then known as the District of Columbia, where it has stayed since.

Did Washington himself put his name in Washington, D.C.?

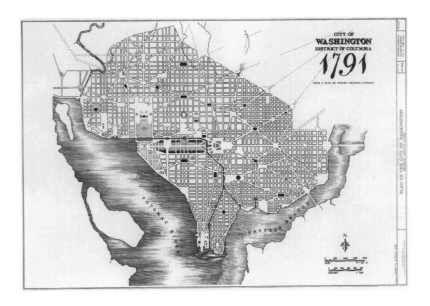

No. In 1791 Congress named the new capital the District of Columbia. The city of Washington was merely a section of the District; it was given its name by the three commissioners who had been appointed to govern the new capital temporarily.

The District of Columbia was originally made up of three separate cities—Georgetown and Washington, on land formerly owned by Maryland, and Alexandria, in former Virginia land. There were three separate city governments. In 1846 Congress returned Alexandria to Virginia, and in 1871 Washington and Georgetown ceased being separate cities. Nowadays the city of Washington is the same thing as the District of Columbia.

HOME SWEET HOME

Washington never lived in the White House. It wasn't completed until 1800, and he left office in 1797. During the years of his presidency, Washington lived in comfortable townhouses in New York City and Philadelphia.

Originally called the President's Palace, the presidential residence was renamed the Executive Mansion in 1810. People were already calling it the White House, but the presidential residence wasn't officially renamed until 1902.

The United States was now free from British domination. Why didn't Washington free the enslaved people under his own domination?

He thought about doing so. By the 1770s he had resolved never to break up a family by buying or selling another slave. In his will he stated that upon Martha's death all of their slaves would be free. And he left money to educate the newly freed young and provide for the elderly.

Washington knew slavery was wrong; he hoped that one day it would be abolished. In a 1786 letter he wrote:

> I never mean (unless some particular circumstance should compel me to it) to possess

another slave by purchase; it being among my first wishes to see some plan adopted, by which slavery in this country may be abolished by slow, sure and imperceptible degrees.

However, he failed to do anything in his private activities or in his role as a public figure to bring about the end of slavery.

He was a product of his time and place, and very few privileged Virginians worked for abolition. Washington and the other Founding Fathers were content to leave future generations the traumatic task of ridding the nation of slavery.

THE SIXTEEN-SIDED BARN

Though as president Washington lived in New York and Philadelphia, he was still involved in the running of Mount Vernon. Always interested in agricultural improvements, in 1792 he designed an innovative sixteen-sided barn for the threshing of wheat.

To separate the grain from the straw, farmers had traditionally either beaten wheat by hand with a *flail* (a sort of large, jointed stick) or had had horses tread upon it outside. Washington's idea was to house the threshing operation in a barn in order to protect the wheat from the weather.

The barn was two stories tall and about fifty-two feet across. Horses walked in circles on the second floor, trampling the wheat. The grain fell through cracks in the floorboards to the first floor, where it was gathered up.

CHAPTER 7

Unrest

The French Revolution by Currier and Ives

Why did Washington agree to a second term in office?

By 1792, the end of Washington's first term, the Federalists, led by Hamilton, and the Republicans, led by Jefferson, were at each other's throats. There was talk in the newspapers of civil war. The president was just about the only man in the entire country whom both sides trusted. Washington was growing weary of the constant strife of politics. He would have much preferred to go home to Mount Vernon. But in order to keep the peace another four years, he agreed to serve a second term.

In October he was, for the second time, elected unanimously by the electoral college.

How did the French Revolution affect America?

Influenced by Enlightenment ideas and the example of the United States, in 1789 the French *bourgeoisie* (meaning, roughly, "middle class" and pronounced, roughly, BURZH-WA-ZEE) decided to stage their own revolution. The people abolished the aristocracy and placed new limits on the Catholic Church.

By 1793 a "Reign of Terror" was under way. Over the course of the next year, more than one thousand "enemies" of the Revolution, including the former King Louis XVI and his wife, Marie Antoinette, were beheaded by the *guillotine*. This device had a heavy, sharp blade that dropped down to chop off the head of the victim. The guillotine was named after the physician who invented it. He thought it was a faster, more humane way to execute people than by hanging.

American sympathies were mixed. Federalists denounced the French revolutionaries as bloodthirsty atheists. Republicans argued that the nobility was only getting what it deserved. The situation became even muddier when Britain declared war on France. Whom should America support—its old ally France, now led by vicious murderers? Or its old enemy Britain, still ruled by the hated and mad King George III?

Washington tried to steer a middle course. Officially the United States remained neutral. The president did everything he could to prevent America from being drawn into the war. And in the end he was successful—the United States fought neither side.

Who was the victor in the clash of titans, Jefferson or Hamilton?

Neither, really, though Hamilton at least managed to remain on good terms with Washington while Jefferson did not.

In late 1793 Jefferson, disappointed by his inability to make Washington see things his way, resigned from the cabinet. Hamilton held out for another year before he, too, resigned. The president had played favorites with neither man, and each was frustrated by his inability to defeat his enemy. Washington mourned the loss of the two brilliant minds, but he must have felt some relief at their departure, too. Less arguing!

What was the Whiskey Rebellion?

In 1794 a new national tax on whiskey angered western frontiersmen. In addition to buying whiskey, Easterners could drink imported rum or wine or make hard cider or beer. But whiskey was the only alcoholic drink readily available in the West. To backwoodsmen the tax was obviously unfair—it was the Stamp Act and the Tea Act all over again. Time to revolt!

Riots broke out in western Pennsylvania, and, at the urging of Alexander Hamilton, Washington called up the militia. Leading a force of 13,000 troops—as many as he had ever commanded in the Revolution—

Washington marched west to put down the rebellion. In the face of overwhelming force, the rioters dispersed. The president had sent a message that the government would not tolerate lawlessness.

What was the Jay Treaty?

Although the Treaty of Paris had secured peace between Britain and the United States, the two nations remained locked in conflict. Britain refused to evacuate seven forts in U.S. territory near the Canadian border. The British navy routinely harassed American merchant ships. And Americans were reluctant to pay pre-war debts to British merchants.

Washington sent the moderate Federalist John Jay of New York to London to negotiate. The problem was that America had little in the way of bargaining chips. If Britain wanted to give America a hard time, there wasn't much America could do about it. Nevertheless, in late 1794 Jay secured a treaty. The terms greatly favored Britain.

Back in America, no one, including Washington, was very happy with the Jay Treaty. Republican newspapers denounced it; in some cities Jay was burned in effigy. But many people, again including Washington, realized that the treaty was probably the best that could be hoped for at the moment. In August 1795 Washington signed a slightly revised version of the treaty, and the next year it was ratified by Congress.

Two years of angry, bitter debate over the Jay Treaty had taken their toll on Washington. He was distressed by the fact that party loyalties had overtaken loyalty to country. He felt that every issue should be decided on its own merits, not by how it appeared to fit in with a political party's ideology.

The fact was, however, that even though Washington would never officially declare himself a Federalist, he had gradually drifted away from the Republicans and toward the Federalists. Republican leaders had criticized Washington mercilessly. They had publicly questioned his honor and his loyalty to the nation. Two terms as president were quite enough. Retirement and Mount Vernon beckoned. He would not serve as president again.

What did Washington say in his Farewell Address?

Washington's Farewell Address is probably his most famous speech, even though it wasn't spoken. It was printed in newspapers across the country. It should be memorable—he worked on it, on and off, for over four years, ever since he had considered retiring after his first term in office.

In the Farewell Address, Washington warned against the destructiveness of party warfare. He believed statesmen should be loyal to the country, not to a political party.

Talented Cousins Across the Sea

The arts were relatively undeveloped in America during the eighteenth century. Here are some of the famous artists and thinkers who lived in Europe during Washington's lifetime.

Jonathan Swift (1667–1745)—Irish author of *Gulliver's Travels*, among many other satirical works

Johann Sebastian Bach (1685–1750)—German composer of fugues, concertos, and church music in the baroque style

Voltaire (1694–1778)—French philosopher, historian, playwright, and poet; leader of the Enlightenment

Samuel Johnson (1709–1784)—English poet, essayist, and dictionary compiler

Jean-Jacques Rousseau (1712–1778)—French philosopher and novelist

Adam Smith (1723–1790)—Scottish philosopher and founder of modern economics

Francisco de Goya (1746–1828)—Spanish painter of dark and somber realistic paintings

Johann Wolfgang von Goethe (1749–1832)—German romantic poet, playwright, novelist, and naturalist

Wolfgang Amadeus Mozart (1756–1791)—Austrian composer of operas, symphonies, and other works in the classical style

William Wordsworth (1770–1850)—English romantic poet

Ludwig van Beethoven (1770–1827) — German composer of classical and romantic symphonies, concertos, and other works

Jane Austen (1775–1817)— English novelist of middle-class manners

He also advised America to avoid "permanent, inveterate antipathies [dislikes] against particular nations and passionate attachments for others." He had in mind, of course, Britain and France. America should be neither permanent enemy nor permanent ally with either. He wanted America to steer clear of European rivalries and entanglements. By staying neutral, the nation could remain independent and strong.

AMERICAN VOICES

❝Though in reviewing the incidents of my administration, I am unconscious of intentional error, I am nevertheless too sensible of my defects not to think it probable that I may have committed many errors. . . . I shall . . . carry with me the hope that my country will never cease to view them with indulgence; and that . . . the faults of incompetent abilities will be consigned to oblivion, as myself must soon be to the mansions of rest. ❞

—**Washington,** in his Farewell Address, 1796

Who was elected president after Washington retired?

In 1796 Washington's vice president, John Adams, running as a Federalist, was narrowly elected president. Washington supported the Federalists against his former friend and fellow Virginian Thomas Jefferson, who received the second-most votes in the electoral college and so won the vice presidency.

CHAPTER 8

First in the Hearts of His Countrymen

A picture of Mount Vernon by Currier and Ives

What did Washington do after retiring from politics?

World famous, the most honored and beloved man of his generation, Washington had become a legend in his own time. After he and Martha returned to Mount Vernon, a constant stream of admirers arrived at his doorstep to pay their respects to the great man.

Meanwhile, Washington went to work. Mount Vernon was in need of repair. The fields and outbuildings required constant care. He rode his property almost every day.

The former president, however, was in his sixties and no longer as strong as he once had been. In 1798 he caught a fever and nearly died. He knew he would probably not live for many more years.

What was the Sedition Act?

After passage of the Jay Treaty, which strengthened ties between the United States and Britain, America's relationship with France deteriorated. Under Napoleon Bonaparte, France's military fortunes improved, and by 1798 the French navy had begun seizing American merchant ships.

President Adams, a Federalist, had little love for France and its Republican sympathizers in America. The Federalists passed the Sedition Act, which made it a crime to "write, print, utter, or publish . . . any false, scandalous, and malicious writing or writings against the government of the United States." The Sedition Act was aimed at Republican critics of the Federalist government.

Washington, still embittered by Republican attacks over the Jay Treaty, at first opposed the Sedition Act but soon came to support it. He didn't believe that the Constitution's guarantee of "freedom of speech" meant that people could say anything they wanted. Republicans had acted irresponsibly; they deserved to be muzzled.

EIGHTEENTH-CENTURY MEDICINE

In Washington's day no one knew that many illnesses were caused by germs—viruses and bacteria. Despite advances in such sciences as chemistry and physics, medicine during the Enlightenment was little different from medieval doctoring.

Physicians treated patients according to a confused mishmash of competing theories. Some doctors considered illness to be a result of weakness in the "life force" of the patient. Others thought disease to be an imbalance in the body's "excitability." Common treatments included opium, alcohol, bloodletting (with leeches or by simply opening a vein), fasting, and sweating. Some doctors even believed mercury—now understood to be a potent poison—could cure disease.

If a patient managed to survive an illness, it was despite, not because of, the doctor's efforts.

Did the Sedition Act succeed in stifling Republican views?

Not really. Public outrage over the Sedition Act probably helped the Republican cause more than the act itself hurt it. Republicans gained control of both Congress and the presidency in 1800. President Jefferson promptly pardoned everyone who had been convicted under the Sedition Act, which itself was allowed to expire the next year.

Why did Washington come out of retirement one last time?

By the summer of 1798 it appeared likely that France would launch an invasion of the United States. In July President Adams asked Washington to lead the army should France attack. Washington accepted and rode to Philadelphia to assume command.

As it happened, France didn't declare war on the United States—Napoleon was too busy fighting Russia, Austria, and Britain. He had enough on his plate without having to fight a war an ocean away.

The crisis passed. In late 1798 Washington left Philadelphia for the last time and returned to Mount Vernon.

TRUE OR FALSE?

Washington wore false teeth made of wood.

False. By the time he was president, Washington had only one tooth left. He did wear false teeth, but they were not wooden. His first set was made out of cow's teeth. Later he had false teeth made out of hippopotamus ivory set in a spring-action metal frame.

True or false? Those must have been some good-looking, comfortable choppers.

False. Like other dentures of the time, Washington's false teeth were unsightly as well as painful to use. No wonder portraits of the president in later life show him to be unsmiling and grim—his teeth looked terrible and his gums ached!

Whatever happened to those giants of Washington's administration, Alexander Hamilton and Thomas Jefferson?

Alexander Hamilton had a special talent for making enemies. Not only did Jefferson despise him, but he also earned the hatred of a man named Aaron Burr, who had served under Washington in the war and later became a political force in New York, Hamilton's home state.

In 1800 Jefferson and Burr received more electoral college votes and defeated John Adams and Charles Pinckney of South Carolina in a closely contested race. But because Burr received the same number of votes as Jefferson, the choice was thrown into the House of Representatives. Amazingly, Jefferson won the 1800 election there, in part thanks to the scheming of his old enemy Hamilton, who wanted to see Burr defeated even more than he wanted to see Jefferson lose. (Jefferson and Burr, too, were enemies—each of the three couldn't stand the others.) In the summer of 1804 the enmity between Hamilton and Burr boiled over, and they met in a duel with pistols. Burr wounded Hamilton, who died the following day.

So—the sitting vice president shot and killed a former secretary of the treasury. Makes today's political rivalries seem like patty cake!

Jefferson went on to serve a second term and is widely considered to have been a great president as well as a brilliant, if erratic, thinker.

Who was Nelly Custis?

George and Martha Washington had no children. But Martha had had a son, Jack, and a daughter, Patsy, with her first husband, Daniel Custis. Patsy had died at seventeen of epilepsy, and Jack had died of typhus at age twenty-six.

Shortly after Jack died, the Washingtons adopted his two younger children, Eleanor and George. Eleanor, known as Nelly, became a special favorite of the president. Raised from infancy at Mount Vernon, Nelly was the child the Washingtons never had. She, in turn, thought of them as the "beloved parents whom I loved with so much devotion, to whose unceasing tenderness I was indebted for every good I possessed."

On February 22, 1799—Washington's last birthday— Nelly Custis married Washington's secretary and nephew, Lawrence Lewis. Three years earlier Washington had advised his step-granddaughter to be cautious when considering whom to marry: "When the fire is beginning to kindle, and your heart growing warm, propound these questions to it. Who is the invader? Have I competent knowledge of him? Is he a man of good character; a man of sense? For be assured a sensible woman can never be happy with a fool."

How did Washington die?

One day Washington went for a ride around Mount Vernon, as was his habit. The day was cold and rainy, and that evening he fell ill with a sore throat. The next day doctors were called for, and

Washington was bled. The treatment may or may not have harmed him, but it certainly didn't help. Washington grew weaker. On the evening of December 14, George Washington died.

How did the nation react to the news of Washington's death?

People throughout the nation went into mourning. Even Republican politicians and writers, who had spent years criticizing the first president, joined in the outpouring of grief. Congress resolved to erect a marble monument in the capital city and recommended that the citizenry wear black armbands for thirty days to mark the president's passing.

ALL IN THE FAMILY

Light-Horse Harry Lee, who served under Washington in the Revolutionary War, was the father of Robert E. Lee, the famous Confederate Army general of the Civil War.

In 1831 Robert E. Lee married Mary Anne Randolph Custis, the only daughter of George Washington Parke Custis, who was in turn the grandson of Martha Washington and the adopted grandson of George Washington.

Washington's eulogy was delivered by his old friend and colleague Henry "Light-Horse Harry" Lee, who summed him up as "a citizen, first in war, first in peace, and first in the hearts of his countrymen."

VOICES FROM HISTORY

❝They wanted me to be another Washington.❞
—**Napoleon Bonaparte**, supposedly, on his deathbed

How was Washington remembered?

Workers on Mount Rushmore

In his lifetime the capital city was named after the man known as "Father of His Country." Thousands of streets, hundreds of schools, dozens of towns and counties—even, in 1889, a state—have been named Washington, too.

After many years of disagreement over the design and funding of the memorial approved by Congress, work finally began on the Washington Monument in 1848. It was delayed by the Civil War, and when the work started again, a different stone was used, giving the monument a two-tone look. It wasn't completed until 1884.

Washington's face is on the one-dollar bill and on the quarter and has been featured on numerous postage stamps. It was sculpted in stone, sixty feet high, on the side of Mount Rushmore.

We celebrate Washington's and Abraham Lincoln's birthdays (Lincoln was born on February 12) jointly on Presidents' Day. Washington's portrait hangs in classrooms all over the country. More than two hundred years after his death, his face is as widely recognized as that of just about anyone in American history.

Furthermore, Washington is remembered in legend—as the boy who never told a lie, as the praying hero of Valley Forge. Many of the legends originated with Parson Weems, but lots of people still believe them today.

How did Parson Weems's biography of Washington affect how people remember him?

Parsons Weems meant well, but he may have harmed Washington's reputation more than he helped it. Weems's Washington—at least that part of him that still survives—is not a flesh-and-blood man but a goody-goody prig. As early as 1853, the famous American author Nathaniel Hawthorne asked, "Did anybody ever see Washington nude? It is inconceivable. He had no nakedness, but I imagine he was born with his clothes on, and his hair powdered, and made a stately bow on his first appearance in the world."

Weems's insistence on Washington's perfection has made the first president seem distant and unreal. Washington's real virtues—his sense of duty and honor, his courage, his modesty and selflessness— are perhaps not those most valued in today's world. It's difficult to feel affection for Washington. The fact that Parson Weems's fictional Washington to a large extent still defines our image of the man doesn't help.

Was George Washington a great general?

A commanding figure

Washington was not a brilliant battlefield tactician, like Napoleon. Even among American generals of the Revolutionary War, he was not considered to be the most skillful commander— his friend General Nathanael Greene probably surpassed him. Washington lost more battles than he won.

Nevertheless, it must be noted that he generally fought with ill-equipped, ill-trained forces. Facing a vastly superior enemy, Washington retreated when necessary and attacked when he could. He avoided disaster. He kept his army together under extremely difficult circumstances. And most important of all— in the end he won.

Was he a great president?

Washington had little formal schooling and was not by nature a deep philosophical or theoretical thinker. He was not a gifted speechmaker. He wasn't a powerful spokesman for a particular political viewpoint, other than the general cause of America's liberty and independence.

On the other hand, as the first president he defined the job. He created the cabinet. He made foreign policy chiefly a presidential, rather than a congressional, task. He declined to make his vice president a very important member of the executive branch.

Most of all, he kept a young and fragile nation at peace for eight critical years. He refused to allow the conflict between Federalists and Republicans to escalate into civil war. He avoided war with both Britain and France. By the time he left office, the nation could survive without him.

Modern historians consistently rank Washington in the top three or four among America's presidents. Many rank him first. If ever there was a great president, Washington was it.

Was he a great man?

An innovative farmer

Washington had a hot temper, which he struggled with, at times unsuccessfully, all his life. He set such high standards for himself that he could be unforgiving of the foibles of others. He had perhaps an undue concern for his own dignity and reputation. His character was not without flaws.

Then there is the question of his holding slaves. He knew it was wrong to keep human beings in bondage, and yet he did so anyway. True, he treated his slaves relatively well, and he refused to break up families by buying or selling people. And he was the only slaveholding president to free his slaves; he instructed Martha to have them released after her death. Still, one wishes Washington had faced up to the contradiction inherent in a slaveholding champion of liberty.

Washington's true greatness lay in his twice giving up power—once when he resigned from the army after Yorktown, when he could have declared himself king, and again when he refused a third term as president. History is full of tyrants and dictators, warlords and conquerors. There have been very few George Washingtons.

As Thomas Jefferson wrote in a letter in 1814:

> Perhaps the strongest feature in [Washington's] character was prudence, never acting until every circumstance, every consideration, was maturely weighed; refraining if he saw a doubt, but, when once decided, going through with his purpose, whatever obstacles opposed. His integrity was most pure, his justice the most inflexible I have ever known. . . . He was, indeed, in every sense of the words, a wise, a good, and a great man.

FEBRUARY 22, 1732	Born in Virginia
1748–50	Accompanies surveying expedition in western Virginia
FALL 1751	Sails to Barbados with older half brother Lawrence
JULY 1752	Lawrence Washington dies
DECEMBER 1752	Becomes a major in the Virginia militia
NOVEMBER 1753– JANUARY 1754	Carries message to commander of French forces in British territory
JANUARY 1754	Publishes account of his adventures carrying message; fame spreads
MARCH 1754	Promoted to lieutenant colonel of the Virginia regiment
MAY 1754	Orders first shots of what would become the French and Indian War
JUNE 1754	Upon the death of Col. Joshua Fry, promoted to colonel
JULY 1754	Defeated at the Battle of Fort Necessity

OCTOBER 1754	Resigns his command in the Virginia regiment
DECEMBER 1754	Leases Mount Vernon from Anne Fairfax Washington, widow of Lawrence Washington; Mount Vernon becomes his permanent home
JULY 1755	Emerges as hero of British General Braddock's failed campaign to take Fort Duquesne
AUGUST 1755	Regains his command in the Virginia regiment
1755–1758	Spends most of his time on the frontier, fighting French and Indians
JULY 1758	Elected to the Virginia House of Burgesses; serves for the next fifteen years
JANUARY 1759	Marries Martha Custis
MARCH 1761	Inherits Mount Vernon plantation when Anne Fairfax Washington dies
APRIL 1764	Parliament passes the Sugar Act
MARCH 1765	Parliament passes the Stamp Act, infuriating the colonies

MARCH 1766	Parliament repeals the Stamp Act
NOVEMBER 1767	The Townshend Revenue Act, placing import duties on lead, paint, paper, glass, and tea, goes into effect
APRIL 1770	Except for the duty on tea, the Townshend Act duties are repealed
APRIL 1773	Parliament passes the Tea Act, further enflaming the colonies
DECEMBER 1773	Boston Tea Party
SEPTEMBER 1774	Attends First Continental Congress as one of seven Virginia delegates
APRIL 1775	Battle of Lexington and Concord
MAY 1775	Attends Second Continental Congress
JUNE 1775	Named supreme commander of continental forces by the Second Continental Congress
MARCH 1776	Drives British out of Boston
JULY 1776	Declaration of Independence
AUGUST–NOVEMBER 1776	Leads army in retreat from New York City

DECEMBER 1776	Crosses Delaware in surprise attack on British forces in New Jersey; Battle of Trenton
JANUARY 1777	Battle of Princeton
SEPTEMBER 1777	Battle of Brandywine Creek; British take Philadelphia
DECEMBER 1777	France enters war on the side of America
WINTER 1777–1778	Winter at Valley Forge
JUNE 1778	British withdraw from Philadelphia; Battle of Monmouth
1778–1780	Endures stalemate with British forces centered in New York City
OCTOBER 1781	Defeats the British at the Battle of Yorktown, effectively ending the Revolutionary War
SEPTEMBER 1783	Treaty of Paris drawn up
DECEMBER 1783	Resigns from the army and returns to Mount Vernon
JANUARY 1784	Treaty of Paris ratified by Congress
MAY–SEPTEMBER 1787	Attends Constitutional Convention
JUNE 1788	Virginia ratifies the Constitution

FEBRUARY 1789	Unanimously elected first president of the United States
APRIL 1789	Sworn in to presidency
DECEMBER 1792	Unanimously reelected president
MARCH 1793	Sworn in to second term
SUMMER 1793	Avoids war with revolutionary France
SEPTEMBER–OCTOBER 1794	Leads militia into western Pennsylvania to put down Whiskey Rebellion
NOVEMBER 1794	John Jay negotiates treaty with Britain
AUGUST 1795	Signs Jay Treaty
SEPTEMBER 1796	Issues Farewell Address
MARCH 1797	Leaves office; John Adams sworn in as new president
MARCH 1797	Retires to Mount Vernon
JULY 1798	Resumes command of United States army in preparation for French attack
DECEMBER 1798	Returns to Mount Vernon for last time
DECEMBER 14, 1799	Dies at Mount Vernon

NONFICTION

Brenner, Barbara. *If You Were There in 1776*. New York: Simon & Schuster, 1994.

Freedman, Russell. *Give Me Liberty! The Story of the Declaration of Independence*. New York: Holiday House, 2000.

Gourley, Catherine. *Welcome to Felicity's World, 1774: Life in Colonial America*. Illustrated by Jamie Young. American Girls Collection. Middleton, Wis.: Pleasant Company, 1999.

Levy, Elizabeth. *If You Were There When They Signed the Constitution*. Illustrated by Joan Holub. New York: Scholastic, 1992.

Meltzer, Milton, ed. *The American Revolutionaries: A History in Their Own Words, 1750–1800*. New York: Crowell, 1987.

Moore, Kay. *If You Lived at the Time of the American Revolution*. Illustrated by Daniel O'Leary. New York: Scholastic, 1998.

FICTION

Avi. *The Fighting Ground*. New York: Harper, 1984.

Denenberg, Barry. *The Journal of William Thomas Emerson: A Revolutionary War Patriot*. My Name Is America Series. New York: Scholastic, 1998.

Gregory, Kristiana. *The Winter of Red Snow: The Revolutionary War Diary of Abigail Jane Stewart, Valley Forge, Pennsylvania, 1777*. Dear America Series. New York: Scholastic, 1996.

Peacock, Louise. *Crossing the Delaware: A History in Many Voices*. Illustrated by Walter Lyon Krudop. New York: Atheneum, 1998.

BOOKS

Alden, John R. *George Washington: A Biography*. New York: Wings Books, 1995.

The American Heritage Book of the Revolution. New York: American Heritage, 1971.

Brookhiser, Richard. *Founding Father: Rediscovering George Washington*. New York: Free Press, 1996.

Colbert, David, ed. *Eyewitness to America: 500 Years of America in the Words of Those Who Saw It Happen*. New York: Pantheon Books, 1997.

Davis, Kenneth C. *Don't Know Much About® History*. New York: Crown, 1990.

Earle, Alison Morse. *Child Life in Colonial Days*. Bowie, Md.: Heritage Classic, 1997.

———. *Home Life in Colonial Days*. Stockbridge, Mass.: Berkshire Traveller Press, 1992.

Fleming, Thomas J., ed. *Affectionately Yours, George Washington: A Self-Portrait in Letters of Friendship*. New York: Norton, 1967.

Garraty, John A., and Peter Gay, eds. *The Columbia History of the World*. New York: Harper & Row, 1972.

Grun, Bernard. *The Timetables of History: A Horizontal Linkage of People and Events*. New York: Simon & Schuster, 1991.

Hawke, David Freeman. *Everyday Life in Early America*. New York: Harper & Row, 1988.

Heffner, Richard D., ed. *A Documentary History of the United States*. 4th ed. New York: New American Library, 1965.

Nye, Russel Blaine. *The Cultural Life of the New Nation, 1776–1830*. New York: Harper, 1960.

The Oxford One-Volume Illustrated Encyclopedia. New York: Oxford University Press, 1997.

Ricks, Christopher, and William L. Vance, eds. *The Faber Book of America.* London and Boston: Faber and Faber, 1992.

Twohig, Dorothy, ed. *George Washington's Diaries: An Abridgment.* Charlottesville: University Press of Virginia, 1999.

Wright, Louis B. *The Cultural Life of the American Colonies, 1607–1763.* New York: Harper, 1957.

Young, Alfred F., et al. *We the People: Voices and Images of the New Nation.* Philadelphia: Temple University Press, 1993.

WEBSITES

Many, many other websites were surfed through, but these were the most helpful.

www.brittanica.com (Encyclopedia Brittanica)

www.digitalhistory.org

www.earlyamerica.com

www.mountvernon.org

www.nara.gov (National Archives)

www.nps.gov (National Park Service)

www.pbs.org

www.xroads.virginia.edu (University of Virginia)